Test-Driven Development with Mockito

Learn how to apply Test-Driven Development and the Mockito framework in real life projects, using realistic, hands-on examples

Sujoy Acharya

BIRMINGHAM - MUMBAI

Test-Driven Development with Mockito

First published: November 2013

Production Reference: 1151113

Published by Packt Publishing Ltd.
Livery Place
35 Livery Street
Birmingham B3 2PB, UK.

ISBN 978-1-78328-329-3

www.packtpub.com

Cover Image by David Studebaker (das189@tigereye.com)

Credits

Author
Sujoy Acharya

Reviewers
Mike Ensor

Daniel Pacak

Acquisition Editor
Rebecca Youe

Commissioning Editor
Neil Alexander

Technical Editors
Shiny Poojary

Akashdeep Kundu

Copy Editors
Alisha Aranha

Roshni Banerjee

Sarang Chari

Janbal Dharmaraj

Tanvi Gaitonde

Sayanee Mukherjee

Alfida Paiva

Project Coordinator
Sherin Padayatty

Proofreader
Saleem Ahmed

Indexer
Priya Subramani

Graphics
Yuvraj Mannari

Production Coordinator
Melwyn D'sa

Cover Work
Melwyn D'sa

About the Author

Sujoy Acharya works as a software architect with Siemens Technology and Services Pvt. Ltd. (STS). He grew up in a joint family and pursued his graduation in the field of computer science and engineering. His hobbies are watching movies, playing outdoor sports, and downloading the latest movies.

He likes to research upcoming technologies. His major contributions are in the fields of Java, J2EE, Web service, Ajax, GWT, and Spring.

He designs and develops healthcare software products. He has over 10 years of industrial experience and has designed and implemented large-scale enterprise solutions.

I would like to thank my wonderful wife, Sunanda, for her patience and endless support in spending many hours reviewing my draft and providing valuable inputs.

I would also like to thank my mother and late father for their support, blessings, and encouragement.

Last, but not the least, I'd like to thank Neha Nagwekar and the Packt Publishing team for their help and valuable inputs.

About the Reviewer

Mike Ensor is a hands-on software architect who has 16 years of experience
in backend development, e-commerce, CMS, distributed systems, and Big Data
implementations. Throughout his career he has continually pushed the use of
test-driven development, and emphasized the merits of agile-based development.
He has been a speaker at past conferences that primarily focusing on implementing
emerging testing strategies during software development. Outside of work, Mike
is an avid ice hockey player, amateur home brewer, world traveler, and enjoys
snowboarding as much as he can.

Daniel Pacak is a self-made Java programmer who fell in love with coding
during his studies of Nuclear Physic at Warsaw University of Technology; it was
in 2006 when no one cared about TDD. He acquired his professional experience
by working on several business-critical projects for clients in the financial services,
telecommunications, e-commerce, and the travel industry.

When he's not coding, he enjoys lifting heavy weights in the gym nearest to his office.

I am very thankful to my parents for their support and the first PC
they sponsored back in 1998. That was when it all started.

www.PacktPub.com

Support files, eBooks, discount offers and more

You might want to visit www.PacktPub.com for support files and downloads related to your book.

Did you know that Packt offers eBook versions of every book published, with PDF and ePub files available? You can upgrade to the eBook version at www.PacktPub.com and as a print book customer, you are entitled to a discount on the eBook copy. Get in touch with us at service@packtpub.com for more details.

At www.PacktPub.com, you can also read a collection of free technical articles, sign up for a range of free newsletters and receive exclusive discounts and offers on Packt books and eBooks.

http://PacktLib.PacktPub.com

Do you need instant solutions to your IT questions? PacktLib is Packt's online digital book library. Here, you can access, read and search across Packt's entire library of books.

Why Subscribe?
- Fully searchable across every book published by Packt
- Copy and paste, print and bookmark content
- On demand and accessible via web browser

Free Access for Packt account holders

If you have an account with Packt at www.PacktPub.com, you can use this to access PacktLib today and view nine entirely free books. Simply use your login credentials for immediate access.

Table of Contents

Preface

Test-Driven Development (**TDD**) is an evolutionary approach to development. It offers test-first development where the production code is written only to satisfy a test. The simple idea of writing a test first reduces the extra effort of writing unit tests after coding.

In Test-Driven Development, test doubles and mock objects are extensively used to mock out external dependencies. Mockito is an open source, unit-testing framework for Java; it allows for the creation, verification, and stubbing of a mock object.

The focus of the book is to provide the readers with comprehensive details on how effectively Test-Driven Development with Mockito can be used for software development. The book begins by giving us an overview of TDD and its implementation. The application of Mockito in TDD is explained in separate chapters. Each chapter provides hands-on examples and step-by-step instructions to develop and execute the code.

What this book covers

This book is about Test-Driven Development and the Mockito framework. Each chapter in this book provides hands-on examples, where we look at how to use TDD and various Mockito features in a step-by-step fashion in detail.

Chapter 1, *Getting Familiar with TDD*, provides an overview on Test-Driven Development, the definition of test, the big picture, and the first TDD example. By the end of this chapter, the reader will be able to understand the core concept of TDD.

Chapter 2, *Refactoring – Roll the Dice*, focuses on getting the reader quickly started with code refactoring and code smells. By the end of this chapter, the reader will be able to identify code smells and refactor the smells.

Chapter 3, Applying TDD, explains the life cycle of TDD and focuses on getting the reader quickly started with Test-Driven Development. By the end of this chapter, the reader will be able to follow the TDD life cycle and write test-first code.

Chapter 4, Understanding the Difference Between Inside-out and Outside-in, explains the commonly used techniques of TDD. By the end of this chapter, the reader will be able to understand the core concept of classical and mockist TDD.

Chapter 5, Test Doubles, illustrates the concept of test doubles. Dummy, Stub, Mock, and Fake doubles are explained in detail. By the end of this chapter, the reader will be able to understand the core concept of Test Doubles.

Chapter 6, Mockito Magic, explains the concept of mock objects using the Mockito framework and provides examples to help the reader understand Mockito APIs. By the end of this chapter, the reader will be able to use Mockito APIs and various features of Mockito.

Chapter 7, Leveraging the Mockito Framework in TDD, explains the advanced features of the Mockito framework, and illustrates usages of Mockito in Test-Driven Development. By the end of this chapter, the reader will be able to use TDD with Mockito.

Chapter 8, World of Patterns, covers the definition and characteristics of a good design, design principles, design patterns, and usages of pattern to refactor code. By the end of this chapter, the reader will be able to identify a bad design and apply the design principle and patterns to refactor the bad design.

Chapter 9, TDD, Legacy Code and Mockito, covers the definition and characteristics of legacy code and provides examples to refactor the legacy code and write unit tests using Mockito. By the end of this chapter, the reader will be able to write unit tests and refactor the legacy code.

Appendix A, TDD Tools and Frameworks, deals with TDD tools and frameworks. It explains the basics of Eclipse and the effective use of keyboard shortcuts to refactor the code and expedite its development; it also explains JUnit 4.0 basics, JUnit 4.0 unit tests, and annotations. By the end of this appendix, the reader will have good understanding of the JUnit 4.0 framework and will be able to smartly use Eclipse using keyboard shortcuts.

Appendix B, Agile Practices, deals with agile concepts and explains continuous integration, provides an example to set up Jenkins to accomplish CIT, and explains the Scrum and Kanban development concepts. By the end of this appendix, the reader will have good understanding of continuous integration and will be able to build an automation using Jenkins and agile development methodology concepts such as Scrum and Kanban.

What you need for this book

You will need the following software to be installed before running the examples:

- Java 5 or higher. JDK 1.5 or higher can be downloaded from the Oracle site: `http://www.oracle.com/technetwork/java/javasebusiness/downloads/java-archive-downloads-javase5-419410.html`.

- An Eclipse editor. The latest version of Eclipse is Kepler (4.3). Kepler can be downloaded from the following site `http://www.eclipse.org/downloads/`.

- Mockito is required for the creation and verification of mock objects, and for stubbing. Mockito can be downloaded from `https://code.google.com/p/mockito/downloads/list`.

Who this book is for

This book is for developers who want to develop software according to Test Driven Development using Mockito and to leverage various Mockito features. Developers don't need prior knowledge of TDD, Mockito, or JUnit.

It is ideal for developers who have some experience in Java application development as well as some basic knowledge of unit testing, but it covers the basic fundamentals of TDD and JUnit testing to get you acquainted with these concepts before you use them.

Conventions

In this book, you will find a number of styles of text that distinguish between different kinds of information. Here are some examples of these styles, and an explanation of their meaning.

Code words in text are shown as follows: "We can include other contexts through the use of the `import` directive."

A block of code is set as follows:

```
public class LoanManager {

    private final LoanCalculator loanCalculator;
    public LoanManager(){
      loanCalculator = new LoanCalculator();
    }
```

```
    public LoanManager(LoanCalculator dependency){
      loanCalculator = dependency;
    }

  public void calculateMaxLoan(Person person){
     loanCalculator.calculate(person);
//other code
    }
  }
```

When we wish to draw your attention to a particular part of a code block, the relevant lines or items are set in bold:

```
@Test(expected=RuntimeException.class)
public void inventory_access_raises_Error() {

when(inventory.getItemsExpireInAMonth()).thenThrow(new
RuntimeException("Database Access fail"));

bazar.issueDiscountForItemsExpireIn30Days(.30);
fail("Code should not reach here");
}
```

New terms and **important words** are shown in bold. Words that you see on the screen, in menus or dialog boxes for example, appear in the text like this: "Clicking on the **Next** button moves you to the next screen".

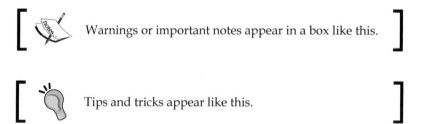

Warnings or important notes appear in a box like this.

Tips and tricks appear like this.

Reader feedback

Feedback from our readers is always welcome. Let us know what you think about this book—what you liked or may have disliked. Reader feedback is important for us to develop titles that you really get the most out of.

To send us general feedback, simply send an e-mail to feedback@packtpub.com, and mention the book title via the subject of your message.

If there is a topic that you have expertise in and you are interested in either writing or contributing to a book, see our author guide on `www.packtpub.com/authors`.

Customer support

Now that you are the proud owner of a Packt book, we have a number of things to help you to get the most from your purchase.

Downloading the example code

You can download the example code files for all Packt books you have purchased from your account at `http://www.packtpub.com`. If you purchased this book elsewhere, you can visit `http://www.packtpub.com/support` and register to have the files e-mailed directly to you.

Errata

Although we have taken every care to ensure the accuracy of our content, mistakes do happen. If you find a mistake in one of our books—maybe a mistake in the text or the code—we would be grateful if you would report this to us. By doing so, you can save other readers from frustration and help us improve subsequent versions of this book. If you find any errata, please report them by visiting `http://www.packtpub.com/submit-errata`, selecting your book, clicking on the **errata submission form** link, and entering the details of your errata. Once your errata are verified, your submission will be accepted and the errata will be uploaded on our website, or added to any list of existing errata, under the Errata section of that title. Any existing errata can be viewed by selecting your title from `http://www.packtpub.com/support`.

Piracy

Piracy of copyright material on the Internet is an ongoing problem across all media. At Packt, we take the protection of our copyright and licenses very seriously. If you come across any illegal copies of our works, in any form, on the Internet, please provide us with the location address or website name immediately so that we can pursue a remedy.

Please contact us at `copyright@packtpub.com` with a link to the suspected pirated material.

We appreciate your help in protecting our authors, and our ability to bring you valuable content.

Questions

You can contact us at questions@packtpub.com if you are having a problem with any aspect of the book, and we will do our best to address it.

1
Getting Familiar with TDD

Test-Driven Development (TDD) is an evolutionary development approach. It offers test-first development where the production code is written only to satisfy a test and refactor.

In this chapter we will look at the following topics:

- Definition of tests
- Examples of TDD
- The big picture
- Steps of TDD

Definition of test

We all go through class tests and medical tests; musicians often check musical instruments before the program. A test is an assessment of our knowledge, a proof of concept, or an examination of data.

A class test is an examination of our knowledge to ascertain whether we can go to the next level. For software, it is the validation of functional and non-functional requirements before it is shipped to customers.

Like other things, Java code can be unit tested using a code-driven unit-testing framework.

The following are a few of the available code-driven unit-testing frameworks for Java:

- SpryTest
- Jtest
- JUnit framework (junit.org)
- TestNG

JUnit is the most popular and widely used unit-testing framework for Java.

In this book, we will be using JUnit 4.0 for unit testing code.

To learn more about JUnit framework, refer to *Appendix A, TDD Tools and Frameworks*.

Object-function programming languages, such as Scala and Groovy, are becoming very popular. They are intended to be compiled as bytecode, and executable code can be run on JVM. Also, they can access Java libraries. Scala/Groovy helps in writing brief, useful tests.

Using Scalatest (http://www.scalatest.org/), you can unit test Scala code as well as Java code.

Usually, developers unit test the code using the main method or by executing the application. Neither of them is the correct approach. Mixing up production code with tests is not a good practice. It creates a code maintainability problem. The best approach is to create a separate source folder for unit tests and put the test class in the same package as the main class. Usually, if a class name is TaxCalculator, its test should have the name TaxCalculatorTest.

Let us write a program to calculate tax for the FY2012-13 and test it.

The rules are as follows:

- If the taxable income is less than USD 500,000, then deduct 10 percent as tax
- The tax is 20 percent for taxable income between USD 500,000 and USD 1,000,000
- The tax is 30 percent for taxable income above USD 1,000,000

So, let us look into the steps that are as follows:

1. Launch Eclipse and create a Java project TDD_With_Mockito. By default, Eclipse will create an empty project with a source folder src. We will add packages and Java files under the src source folder. But, as mentioned in the preceding section, the best practice is to have a separate source folder for unit tests. We will add all our unit tests under the test source folder.

2. To create a source folder `test`, right-click on the project. Eclipse will open a pop-up menu. Expand the **New** menu and click on the **Source Folder** menu item. It will open the **New Source Folder** pop-up. In the **Folder Name** textbox, enter `test` and hit the **Finish** button. It will add the `test` source folder.

3. Now add a new JUnit 4.0 test `TaxCalculatorTest` in the `test` folder. To execute unit tests, Eclipse needs the JUnit library in the classpath, so Eclipse will recommend adding the JUnit 4.0 library to the classpath. You can accept the recommendation or manually add the JUnit library to the classpath.

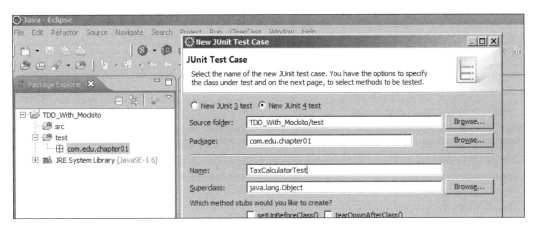

Add a test to verify the first rule that the tax is 10 percent when the taxable income is less than USD 500,000.

4. Create a `public void` method `when_income_less_than_5Lacs_then_ deducts_10_percent_tax ()` in `TaxCalculatorTest.java`. Annotate the method with the `@test` annotation. JUnit 4.0 needs this annotation to identify a test:

```
@Test
public void when_income_less_than_5Lacs_then_deducts_10_percent_
tax() {

}
```

For tests, we will follow the convention: `when_some_condition is met_ then_this_happens`.

We will use underscores (underscore in a method name is not recommended for production code) for test methods.

5. In this test method, write `new TaxCalculator()`. The compiler will complain that the class doesn't exist. Press *Ctrl + 1*; Eclipse will suggest the creation of a `TaxCalculator` class. Select the option and create the class in the `com.edu.chapter01` package under the `src` source folder.

6. We have the calculator class ready! Now we need to add a method that will take the total taxable income as an input and return the payable tax amount. Write `double payableTax = taxCalculator.calculate(400000.00);` and the compiler will tell you that this method doesn't exist. Press *Ctrl+1* and select **Create method calculate(double) in type 'TaxCalculator'**.

7. Our API is ready. We need to verify that this method returns 10 percent of 400,000. To do that, we have to take the help of the JUnit framework. We will assert the expected and actual values. Write `assertTrue (40000 == payableTax);`.

> The `org.junit.Assert` class provides a set of static assertion methods. We can statically import any method we need.
>
> assertEquals(expected, actual) is a method that takes two values: expected and actual. If actual calculated value doesn't match the expected value, it throws an exception and the test fails. It indicates that there is something wrong in the calculation.
>
> We should have used this method here. But `assertEquals` is deprecated for double values. So, to verify an expected double, we will not use this deprecated method. For any other data type, `assertEquals` is the best choice.
>
> We can use BigDecimal instead of the primitive double. BigDecimal is recommended for double value calculation, such as subtraction and multiplication.

8. Run the test (press *Alt + Shift + X* then *T*). The test will fail. The `calculate()` method returns **0**. Open the `TaxCalculator` class and change the `calculate()` method to return 40,000, that is, 10 percent of USD 400,000. Save the file and run the test. Bingo! It works. The following is the test:

```
@Test
public void when_income_less_than_5Lacs_then_deducts_10_percent_
tax() {
    TaxCalculator taxCalculator = new TaxCalculator();
    double payableTax = taxCalculator.calculate(400000.00);
    assertTrue(40000 == payableTax);
}
```

Following is the code snippet:

```
public class TaxCalculator {
    public double calculate(double taxableIncome) {
```

```
        return 40000;
    }

}
```

9. Now check the boundary values 0 and 500,000. Modify the `test` method and call the `calculate` method with 0 and 500,000.

```
@Test
public void when_income_less_than_5Lacs_then_deducts_10_percent_
tax() {
    TaxCalculator taxCalculator = new TaxCalculator();
    double payableTax = taxCalculator.calculate(400000.00);
    assertTrue(40000 == payableTax);

    payableTax = taxCalculator.calculate(0);
    assertTrue(0 == payableTax);

    payableTax = taxCalculator.calculate(500000.00);
    assertTrue(50000 == payableTax);

}
```

Run the test.

The test fails because it expects 0, but the actual method returns 40,000.
If we return 0 from `calculate()`, it will fail the 40,000 data condition; if we
return 50,000, then it will fail 40,000 and 0, that is, both conditions. So for the
three test conditions, we need three values — 40,000, 0, and 50,000. Returning
40,000 from the `calculate` method causes this test failure. It seems we
need to return 10 percent of the taxable income. Add this condition to our
`calculate()` method.

The code will look something like this:

```
public class TaxCalculator {
    public double calculate(double taxableIncome) {
        return (taxableIncome / 10);
    }

}
```

Rerun the test. It will pass. So we covered a random value and two boundary
value conditions.

10. Now, write another test and enter any amount greater than 500,000 as an input to the `calculate()` method. Oops! The test fails! We need to return 20 percent above 500,000 and 10 percent below USD 500,000. Change the code to return 20 percent of USD 300,000 and 10 percent of USD 500,000.

```
@Test
public void when_income_between_5lacs_and_10lacs_then_deducts_
fifty_thousand_plus_20_percent_above_5lacs() {
  TaxCalculator taxCalculator = new TaxCalculator();
  double payableTax = taxCalculator.calculate(800000.00);
  double expectedTaxForFirstFiveHundredThousand = 50000;
  double expectedTaxForReminder = 60000;
  double expectedTotalTax =
    expectedTaxForFirstFiveHundredThousand +
      expectedTaxForReminder;
  assertTrue(expectedTotalTax  == payableTax);
}
```

Change the `calculate()` method to return 110,000:

```
public class TaxCalculator {
  public double calculate(double taxableIncome) {
    return 110000;
  }
}
```

Our new test runs fine, but the existing tests are broken. So, reverse the change. We need to return 10 percent of the taxable income when the amount is less than 500,000, otherwise the test will return 110,000.

```
public class TaxCalculator {
  public double calculate(double taxableIncome) {
    if(taxableIncome > 500000){
      return 110000;
    }
    return (taxableIncome / 10);
  }
}
```

11. Everything is green. All tests are proving the concept. It's time to test some other value. We will try USD 900,000. The test will fail since it doesn't get the expected value; instead `calculate` returns 110,000. We need to add code to return 20 percent above USD 500,000

```
public class TaxCalculator {
  public double calculate(double taxableIncome) {
    if(taxableIncome > 500000){
      return 50000+((taxableIncome-500000)/5);
    }
    return (taxableIncome / 10);
```

```
    }
}
```

Yes, it is working for both the tests! Add another test to work with income greater than USD 1,000,000.

What we just completed is TDD.

Kent Beck is the originator of Extreme Programming and TDD. He has authored many books and papers. Please visit the following link for details:

```
http://en.wikipedia.org/wiki/Kent_Beck
```

TDD gives us the following benefits:

- Clean, testable, and maintainable code.
- Another benefit to incrementally building your code is that your API is easier to work with, because the code is written and used at the same time.
- When we document our code, and then update the code but forget to update the documentation, it creates confusion. You can document your code and keep it updated or write your code and unit tests in such a way that anybody can understand the intent. In TDD, tests are written to provide enough documentation of code. So, the test is our documentation, but we need to clean the tests too in order to keep them readable and maintainable.
- We can write many tests with boundary value conditions, zero, negative numbers, and so on, and verify our code. You are trying to break your own code as soon as possible. There is no need to package the whole application and ship it to **quality assurance (QA)** or the customer to discover issues.
- You should also avoid over engineering the class that you are writing. Just write what's needed to make all tests green.

The big picture

It doesn't matter how small or big a project is; every project has an architecture. An architect (or designer) takes design decisions to satisfy the functional goal of the project and normalizes non-functional requirements, such as security, availability, performance, and scalability. In this process, different components of the system and interaction between these components are identified.

For example, health provider organizations (hospitals) provide care 24/7, so the patient check-in software needs to be available at all times. Also, it needs to communicate with insurance companies to validate policy information, send claims, and receive remittances. Here, the architecture should define the different components of the system, the protocol to communicate with insurance companies, and how to deploy the system so that it complies 24/7.

For testing architecture, unless the code is ready for testing, you cannot test quality attributes and functionality. What if during testing we find the communication protocol we defined is wrong? All the effort of architecture and coding is wasted.

It is not wise to put months of effort in the architecture; cards, sequence diagrams, and models are essential to represent the architecture, but only drawing conceptual diagrams doesn't help. Before the construction phase, the baseline architecture needs to be provided to the development team. While building this baseline architecture, write testable code, identify problems, and attack them quickly. If anything goes wrong, that can be fixed early.

We all often have trouble believing our own code is broken. In the traditional waterfall approach, the developers write the code and pass the completed development to the software testers. The testers try to break the system and find bugs!

TDD helps a lot here. The flow is the reverse of conventional flow and iterative.

The following are the steps involved in TDD:

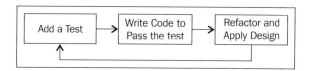

A test is written for a requirement, a code is added to pass the test, the code is cleaned, and the design is identified. Then again another test is added; this process continues.

Refactoring

The third step of TDD is refactoring. Let us revisit the code we wrote for TaxCalculator:

```
public class TaxCalculator {

    public double calculate(double taxableIncome) {
        if(taxableIncome > 1000000){
            return 150000 + (((taxableIncome-1000000)*30)/100);
```

```
    }

    if(taxableIncome > 500000){
      return 50000+((taxableIncome-500000)/5);
    }

    return (taxableIncome / 10);
  }

}
```

The tests are running fine but the code looks ugly. It is not readable. What is `150000 + (((taxableIncome-1000000)*30)/100)`? Extract methods to explain the intent of the code. Create two methods `isIncomeIn30PercentTaxRange`(...) and `isIncomeIn20PercentTaxRange`(..) to check the amount greater than 1,000,000 and 500,000 respectively. Replace conditions with methods. And rerun the tests. If any test fails, then immediately reverse the code. Change and identify the root cause.

```
public double calculate(double taxableIncome) {
  if(isIncomeIn30PercentTaxRange(taxableIncome)){
    return 150000 + (((taxableIncome-1000000)*30)/100);
  }

  if(isIncomeIn20PercentTaxRange(taxableIncome)){
    return 50000+((taxableIncome-500000)/5);
  }

  return (taxableIncome * .10);
}
```

Still not readable! When taxable income is more than 1,000,000, deduct 30 percent above 1,000,000 and for an amount less than 1,000,000, apply another strategy. This can be represented using the following code:

```
public double calculate(double taxableIncome) {
  if(isIncomeIn30PercentTaxRange(taxableIncome)){
    return deduct30PercentAbove10Lacs(taxableIncome) +
      calculate(1000000);
  }

  if(isIncomeIn20PercentTaxRange(taxableIncome)){
    return deduct20PercentAbove5Lacs(taxableIncome) +
      calculate(500000);
  }

  return (taxableIncome * .10);
}
```

```
protected double deduct20PercentAbove5Lacs(double taxableIncome) {
    return (taxableIncome-500000)*.20;
}

protected double deduct30PercentAbove10Lacs(double taxableIncome) {
    return (taxableIncome-1000000)*.30;
}
```

Now the code is more readable and maintainable. This process is known as **Refactoring**. We will explore more of this in the next chapter.

Summary

In this chapter we read about TDD, practiced test-first development, and covered the TDD big picture.

By now, the reader will be able to understand the core concept of TDD.

Chapter 2, Refactoring – Roll the Dice, focuses on getting the reader quickly started with code refactoring and code smells.

2
Refactoring – Roll the Dice

Refactoring is restructuring code to improve readability, maintainability, and extensibility.

In this chapter we will look at the following topics:

- Definition of refactoring
- Refactoring examples
- Code smells
- Starting and stopping refactoring

Refactoring

Refactoring is a series of small steps to change the internal structure of code without altering its external behavior. Refactoring is applied to make the code readable, maintainable, and clean.

Reasons behind refactoring

Refactoring is required to achieve the following points:

- **Easy to add new features/code**: Design erodes very quickly. Developers add features and hack the design to accomplish short-term goals. Refactoring helps in maintaining the design.

- **Improves the design of the existing code**: Open/closed, DRY, and YAGNI are very useful design principles. If any piece of code violates them, refactor the code.

  - **DRY**: This principle means Don't Repeat Yourself. If a class has a duplicate code, it violates the DRY principle. If we find any bug in the duplicate code, we have to fix the same code in all places. It removes code duplication—so bug fixing is easy now.

  - **Open/closed**: This principle states that a piece of code should be open for extension but closed for modification, that means the design should be done in such a way that a new functionality should be added with minimum changes in the existing code.

  - **YAGNI**: This principle refers to over engineering. The full form of YAGNI is You Aren't Gonna Need It. Add code for today's feature, not for tomorrow.

- **Improves readability and understanding**: If you don't understand the code, maintenance becomes a nightmare. Removing duplicates and dead code, giving proper names to methods and classes, removing unnecessary comments, making short methods and small classes, delegating responsibilities of a *GOD* object to other classes, applying a proper design pattern to conserve the open/closed principle, and so on make code clean and easy to change.

Refactoring schedule

It is important to know when we can start refactoring; following are the triggering points:

- Adding a new feature: To add a new feature to an existing code, it is necessary to understand the code. If you don't understand the intent of the code/design or if the code is too complex to change/add a new feature, immediately start refactoring.

- Fixing bug: Fixing bugs? Look for code smells and start refactoring.

- During code review: Code review helps to improve the code. Many times I found that I missed something in the design and caught it at the time of code reviewing. It also improves reviewers' knowledge. So, during code review, if you find anything annoying, immediately start refactoring.

When not to refactor

We read about the triggers of refactoring and the reasons for refactoring, but we must also know when not to refactor. The following points describe the situations when we should *not* continue refactoring:

- Code does not work: When an application is broken, it is unwise to start or continue refactoring, unless the functionalities are back online.

- Not enough tests: We can refactor a code with confidence when we have supporting tests. If anything goes wrong during refactoring, tests will raise errors and alert us that we broke something. If a piece of code is not well covered by unit tests, do not refactor it.

- Rewrite: When the code is too fragile! We need to estimate which one is easier: rewrite or refactor?

Stopping refactoring

It's tricky to know when to stop refactoring; software quality improvement is an ongoing process, always there is plenty of scope for improvement, but we cannot refactor forever. Remember the core agile principle of *good enough*. Following are the conditions of when to stop refactoring:

- All tests are green

- Class and method names are meaningful

- No code duplication (the code uses the smallest number of classes and methods)

- Each class is doing its own work; if needed, it delegates work to other classes

- No bidirectional dependencies—A > B and B > A

- Moreover, the code expresses the purpose

- Finally, adding a new feature is not causing cascading changes in all layers/modules

Look at the following class `OnceYouBuyYouStartCryingTelephone` and try to understand the purpose of this class:

```java
public class OnceYouBuyYouStartCryingTelephone {
    public static final int TWO_G = 2;
    public static final int THREE_G = 3;
    public static final int FOUR_G = 4;
    private Map<String, String> names = new HashMap<String,
      String>();
```

```
    private Map<String, Integer> types = new HashMap<String,
        Integer>();
    private Map<String, Date> cd = new HashMap<String, Date>();


    /**
```

This method activates a connection for a customer and stores different information in following maps for future use names, types and **cd**. if the connection type is 2G then requests TRY for a valid 2G number. if portability is not an issue then TRY provides a valid number, that number is stored for the customer. Then we activate the connection. For 3G - user needs **data plan** , we **don't** ask TRY for 3G...we **don't** have permission for 3G data in many cities, so we will hack TRY database and assign an id. If TRY catches us then we will disconnect the **data plan** and **deactivate** the customer.

 Is there any legal consumer forum issue?
 For 4G- we **don't** have 4th generation spectrum. we will provide 3G with a wrapper of 4G

```
      * @param a
      * @param s
      * @param b
      * @param c
      * @param z
      * @param gen
      * @return
      **/
    public String add(String a, String s, String b,
      String c, Date z, int gen) {
        if (a == null || c == null || z == null)
            throw new RuntimeException();
        String r = "";
        if (s != null) {
            r = r + " " + s;
            if (a != null)
                r = r + " " + a;
            if (b != null)
                r = r + " " + b;
            if (c != null)
                r = r + c;
        } else {
            if (a != null)
                r = r + " " + a;
            if (b != null)
                r = r + " " + b;
            if (c != null)
```

```
                r = r + c;
        }

        String n = Number.next();

        names.put(n, r);
        cd.put(n, z);

        if (gen == TWO_G) {
            activate2GCon(n);
            types.put(n, TWO_G);
        } else if (gen == THREE_G) {
            activate3GCon(n);
            types.put(n, THREE_G);
        } else if (gen == FOUR_G) {
            activate4GCon(n);
            types.put(n, FOUR_G);
        } else {
            throw new IllegalStateException();
        }

        return n;
    }

    /**
     * This method takes number as input and generates post paid bills
     * @param n
     * @return
     **/
    public String bill(String n) {
        Integer gen = types.get(n);
        if (gen == null) {
            throw new RuntimeException();
        }
        switch (gen.intValue()) {
        case TWO_G:
            return gen2GBill(n);
        case THREE_G:
            return gen3GBill(n);
        case FOUR_G:
            return gen4GBill(n);

        default:
            break;
```

```
        }
        return "";
    }

    public void chargeIncomingSms(String num) {
        //code....
        //....
    }
```

This class has the following characteristics:

- An add() method with a long argument list.
- The add() method accepts single-character variables. What is the purpose of String a?
- Method name add() doesn't tell you the intent of the method. Does it add numbers?
- The add() method is doing many things, single-character variables are participating in some calculation, nested if conditions.
- add() has a a twenty-line-long documentation. Is it a code documentation or business strategy documentation? Does it describe the add() method?
- There is a private class-level variable cd. What is cd? Compact disk? Seems like no one is using it.
- There is a bill() method. bill() has nested if conditions similar to those in the add() method.
- The class is adding something that we don't understand, generating bills, and charging for incoming text messages.

As per the refactoring guidelines, this class has the following issues:

- Not readable, therefore, not maintainable.
- Duplicate code and nested if conditions in the add() and bill() methods.
- The class is doing many things—GOD object. The add() method is also doing many things.
- The add() method is very long.
- Unnecessary comments are present.
- The class is violating the open-close principle. A new enhancement will touch almost all methods in this class.
- Finally, the class doesn't have JUnits.

To make the code readable, we will carry out the following steps:

1. First, write a few tests and check the method output for different inputs.
2. Then try to make the code readable.
3. Re-run the tests. They will ensure that the functionality is not changed.

Let us apply the following steps:

1. We will create a **OnceYouBuyYouStartCryingTelephone**.java class under the com.packtpub.chapter02 package and copy the code to this class.

2. Add a test class com.packtpub.chapter02. **OnceYouBuyYouStartCryingTelephoneTest** under the test source folder. Here, we will start with the add() method. With some code analysis, we can determine that the input values for a, c, z, and **gen** are mandatory because the method will throw an exception if any of the three string values are null or gen is not 2,3, or 4. Let's write some tests to cover these conditions by passing in null for each variable and asserting the exception.

```
OnceYouBuyYouStartCryingTelephone telephone = new
OnceYouBuyYouStartCryingTelephone();

    @Test(expected=RuntimeException.class)
    public void when_input_a_is_null_then_throws_exception()
throws Exception {
        telephone.add(null, null, null, null, null, 0);
        fail("code should not reach here");
    }


    @Test(expected=RuntimeException.class)
    public void when_input_c_is_null_then_throws_exception()
throws Exception {
        telephone.add("a", null, null, null, null, 0);
        fail("code should not reach here");
    }


    @Test(expected=RuntimeException.class)
    public void when_input_z_is_null_then_throws_exception()
throws Exception {
        telephone.add("a", null, null, "c", null, 0);
        fail("code should not reach here");
    }


    @Test(expected=RuntimeException.class)
    public void when_input_gen_is_invalid_then_throws_exception()
throws Exception {
```

```
        telephone.add("a", null, null, "c", new Date(), 0);
        fail("code should not reach here");
    }


    @Test
    public void when_valid_input_then_adds_inputs() throws
Exception {
        assertNotNull(telephone.add("a", null, null, "c", new
Date(), OnceYouBuyYouStartCryingTelephone.THREE_G));


    }
```

3. The add() method is building a message from strings a, s, b, and c and then putting it to name map. So, looks like it is building a name from four strings. Variables a and c are mandatory. The variables a and c could be first and last name, b could be null and added between a and c. So, b is a middle name and s is a prefix. That's fine, but how could we test this? Okay, the bill() method generates bills with names. We have to call the bill() method to test the name. Also, the add() method is returning a string, which is generated from the Number object. So add() is generating a number:

```
@Test
public void when_all_name_attributes_are_passed_then_forms_the_
name()
            throws Exception {
    String johnsFirstName = "john";
    String johnsLastName = "smith";
    String johnsMiddleName = "maddison";
    String johnsNamePrefix = "dr.";

String number = telephone.add(johnsFirstName,
johnsNamePrefix,johnsMiddleName,
johnsLastName, new Date(),
            OnceYouBuyYouStartCryingTelephone.FOUR_G);

    assertNotNull(number);
    String billDetails = telephone.bill(number);
    assertTrue(billDetails.contains(johnsNamePrefix));
    assertTrue(billDetails.contains(johnsLastName));
    assertTrue(billDetails.contains(johnsMiddleName));
    assertTrue(billDetails.contains(johnsFirstName));
}
```

4. Now we have the test. So, we can start removing noises. First, change the method argument `a` to `firstName` and replace all references of `a` with `firstName`.

5. Then, run the tests to make sure nothing is broken. If the tests run fine, take another argument and change the name. It should look like the following code:

```
public String add(String firstName, String prefix, String
           middleName, String lastName, Date z, int gen) {
        if (firstName == null || lastName == null || z ==
          null)
            throw new RuntimeException();
        String personName = "";
        if (prefix != null) {
            personName = personName + " " + prefix;
            if (firstName != null)
                personName = personName + " " + firstName;
            if (middleName != null)
                personName = personName + " " + middleName;
            if (lastName != null)
                personName = personName + lastName;
        } else {
            if (firstName != null)
                personName = personName + " " + firstName;
            if (middleName != null)
                personName = personName + " " + middleName;
            if (lastName != null)
                personName = personName + lastName;
        }
```

6. Well, the method name `add()` doesn't tell you anything about the objective of the method. We can rename it to `addConnection()`. Select the `add()` method and hit *Alt + Shift + R*, then enter the new name and hit *Enter*. It will rename the method and replace all the `add()` references with the new name. Revisit the test. Tests are still holding names such as `a` and `c`. Refactor the tests to have proper names such as `when_input_first_name_is_null...()`.

What we have done here is called refactoring. We should always look at our code and grasp the possible refactoring opportunities. Refactoring makes the code healthy and clean.

Google™ contributed an Eclipse plugin, CodePro AnalytiX™, to generate tests from existing code, code health check-ups, and many more useful things. This is a great tool to have. This can be downloaded from the following link:

```
https://developers.google.com/java-dev-tools/codepro/
doc/?csw=1
```

Now we will learn about code smell, and refactor the preceding example in the shed of code smell.

Code smell

Code smell is an indication that something is wrong in the code. *Kent Beck* introduced this term. Smells are indication that you need refactoring.

By looking at a piece of code, how can one say if it stinks or not? Experts researched many projects, million lines of code, and came up with a catalogue of smells. For a detailed list, please visit the following link:

```
http://c2.com/cgi/wiki?CodeSmell
```

The examples of code smell are described in the following sections.

Switch statements

The `switch (case)` statement and nested `if` conditions (`if`, `else if`, and so on) are an essential part of decision making. But they become ugly when we add many cases or many levels of `if-else-if`. It makes our design complex, reduces readability, and violates the open/closed principle. Often we copy the same `switch` statement in different classes and create conceptual code duplications.

In the preceding refactoring example, we found that duplicate nested `if` conditions are present in both `addConnection()` and `bill()` methods. They are conceptual duplicates. This can be refactored by applying polymorphic behavior (**strategy pattern**).

Create an interface called `PhoneConnection` and define the required methods, `activate(String connectionForUserName, String number)` and `generateBillFor(String number)`.

```
public interface PhoneConnection {
    boolean activate(String connectionForUserName, String number);
    String generateBillFor(String number);
}
```

Create an enum called ConnectionType to define the possible connection types—such as 2G, 3G, or 4G. If a new connection type is required, we just need to add a constant in the ConnectionType enum:

```
public enum ConnectionType {
  TWO_G(), THREE_G(), FOUR_G();
}
```

Implement the PhoneConnection interface and provide specific behavior.

Create a class for 2G connections. Call it TwoGConnection. It has to implement the activate and genearteBillFor methods. Just copy the content of the activate2GCon(...) method to the activate(...) method and gen2GBill() to generateBillFor().

Wait a second, gen2GBill() accesses a class-level variable named map, which is set from the addConnection() method. We will copy this map variable to the new class, set the username from the activate() method, and access it from the generateBillFor() method:

```
public class TwoGConnection implements PhoneConnection {
    private Map<String, String> numberAndNameMap = new
      HashMap<String, String>();
    @Override
    public boolean activate(String connectionForUserName, String
      number) {
       System.out.println("activating 2G for
         user="+connectionForUserName+"and number=" +number);
       numberAndNameMap.put(number, connectionForUserName);
       return true;
    }

    @Override
    public String generateBillFor(String number) {
        return "2G bill for "+numberAndNameMap.get(number);
    }

}
```

Similarly, define a ThreeGConnection class:

```
public class ThreeGConnection implements PhoneConnection {

    private Map<String, String> numberAndNameMap = new
      HashMap<String, String>();
    @Override
```

```
public boolean activate(String connectionForUserName, String
  number) {
    System.out.println("activationg 3G for
      user="+connectionForUserName+"and number=" +number);
    numberAndNameMap.put(number, connectionForUserName);
    return true;
}

@Override
public String generateBillFor(String number) {
    return "3G bill for "+numberAndNameMap.get(number);
}

}
```

Now, modify the OnceYouBuyYouStartCryingTelephone class, add a map variable to hold ConnectionType and PhoneConnection, and add a void method initialize to populate the map. Here, initialize the map with all connection types and their implementations, as shown in the following code:

```
private Map<ConnectionType, PhoneConnection> connectionForATypeMap
= new HashMap<ConnectionType, PhoneConnection>();
public OnceYouBuyYouStartCryingTelephone(){
    initialize();
}

protected void initialize() {
    connectionForATypeMap.put(ConnectionType.TWO_G,
new TwoGConnection());
    connectionForATypeMap.put(ConnectionType.THREE_G,
new ThreeGConnection());
}
```

We will explain the preceding code later.

Modify the addConnection() method so that it passes a ConnectionType instance of enum type instead of an int argument gen. This will break all tests. Fix the tests by passing enum-type.

We have a compilation error in the addConenction() method. Nested if conditions will fail to compile. It expects a number but gets a ConnectType instance of type enum. Remove the nested if conditions and replace them with the following piece of code:

```
String n = Number.next();
```

```
        names.put(n, personName);
        cd.put(n, z);

        PhoneConnection connection =
    connectionForATypeMap.get(connectionType);

        if (connection == null) {
            throw new IllegalStateException();
        }
        connection.activate(personName, n);
```

What we have done here is made the class open for extension and close for modification. Now, if we add a new connection type, we don't have to touch the addConnection() method. We only need to add a constant in the enum type and an implementation class for that new connection type.

Run the tests. Everything will work except a test. Bill generation still has the nested if conditions.

This method asks a map variable to get the connection type for a number, which we removed along with the nested if conditions in the addConenction() method. We have to create a map of number and ConenctionType and set it from the addConnection() method. Also, we no longer need the names map. We moved the names map to the implementation classes. Now, the addConnection() method will look like the following code:

```
public String addConnection(String firstName, String prefix, String
    middleName, String lastName, Date z, ConnectionType connectionType) {
        if (firstName == null || lastName == null || z == null)
            throw new RuntimeException();
        String personName = "";
        if (prefix != null) {
            personName = personName + " " + prefix;
            if (firstName != null)
                personName = personName + " " + firstName;
            if (middleName != null)
                personName = personName + " " + middleName;
            if (lastName != null)
                personName = personName + lastName;
        } else {
            if (firstName != null)
                personName = personName + " " + firstName;
            if (middleName != null)
                personName = personName + " " + middleName;
            if (lastName != null)
```

```
                    personName = personName + lastName;
            }

            String number = Number.next();

            connectionTypeForNumberMap.put(number, connectionType);
            cd.put(number, z);

            PhoneConnection connection =
              connectionForATypeMap.get(connectionType);

            if (connection == null) {
                throw new IllegalStateException();
            }
            connection.activate(personName, number);

            return number;
        }
```

Now, modify the nested `if` conditions in the `bill` method:

```
    public String bill(String number) {
            ConnectionType connectionType =
                connectionTypeForNumberMap.get(number);

            if (connectionType == null) {
                throw new RuntimeException();
            }

    PhoneConnection connection =
          connectionForATypeMap.get(connectionType);

            return connection.generateBillFor(number);
        }
```

See, the `bill()` method is so simple now. The test will pass.

So one way to overcome nested `if` conditions issue is **polymorphism** and strategy patterns.

Duplicate code

Duplicate code is the stinky kind. It means the same code structure is present in more than one place in a program. Duplicate code could be either of the following two types:

- copy-paste duplicate
- conceptual duplication

Duplicate code violates the DRY principle—Don't Repeat Yourself. If any bug is found in a duplicate code, the developer has to fix it in all places.

Revisit the code we have in the `addConnection()` method. We removed the conceptual duplication from `addConnection()` and `bill()` by employing strategy patterns. But still we have duplicate code:

```
String personName = "";
     if (prefix != null) {
          personName = personName + " " + prefix;
          if (firstName != null)
               personName = personName + " " + firstName;
          if (middleName != null)
               personName = personName + " " + middleName;
          if (lastName != null)
               personName = personName + lastName;
     } else {
          if (firstName != null)
               personName = personName + " " + firstName;
          if (middleName != null)
               personName = personName + " " + middleName;
          if (lastName != null)
               personName = personName + lastName;
     }
```

The same code is repeated to build a person name (as highlighted in the preceding code).

To remove the duplicate, extract the common code, select the highlighted portion of the code, and hit *Alt + Shift + M*. It will ask for a method name; enter `buildName()`.

Modify the method into the following:

```
protected String buildName(String firstName, String middleName,
        String lastName) {
    StringBuilder personName = new StringBuilder();
    if (firstName != null) {
        personName.append(firstName).append(" ");
    }
    if (middleName != null) {
        personName.append(middleName).append(" ");
    }
    if (lastName != null) {
        personName.append(lastName);
    }
    return personName.toString();
}
```

Change `addConenction()` to use this method and don't use `String` for the concatenation operation as it creates multiple objects. Instead use a `StringBuilder` class instance:

```
    StringBuilder personName = new StringBuilder();
if (prefix != null) {
    personName.append(prefix).append(" ");
}

    personName.append(
        buildName(firstName, middleName, lastName));
```

Wait a minute! Should it not be the responsibility of `buildName()` to return a name? Why do we need to append a name with a prefix? The `buildName()` method should take care of this. It should take all four parameters and return a name:

```
public String addConnection(String firstName, String prefix,
        String middleName, String lastName, Date z,
        ConnectionType connectionType) {
    if (firstName == null || lastName == null || z == null)
        throw new RuntimeException();

    String personName = buildName(prefix, firstName,
middleName, lastName);

    }
```

Are we missing anything? Yes. Check the `TwoGConnection` and `ThreeGConnection` classes. They have the same variable defined for storing the username. You can refactor that by creating an abstract class and moving the map to that class and 2G/3G will extend this class and access the map variable.

Also, the `Template` method can be used (common methods can be moved to a super class and to provide a hook to the subclasses). Different subclasses will inherit from the base class and either implement the hooks or leave it.

So, duplication can be refactored using extracting methods, templates, and **aspect-oriented programming**. Visit the following link for further details on aspect-oriented programming:

`http://en.wikipedia.org/wiki/Aspect-oriented_programming`

Comments

> *"Don't comment bad code – rewrite it."*
>
> *-Kernighan and Plaugher*

Comment is another smell. Our `addConnection()` method doesn't need any comment. It will be cleaner. It may stop supporting 2G connections in the future, but we will not update the comment to remove the reference of 2G. Comments are never updated.

Sometimes we comment out code and forget to remove them. Always remove unused, commented-out code—they create confusion.

Long methods and parameter list

Long methods are error prone. When you see 200 lines of code in a method, it becomes almost impossible to maintain the method. It violates the **single responsibility principle** 99 percent of the time.

The best way to resolve this is by extracting small methods and calling them. Each method does only one thing. But the problem with this approach is if we need to pass too many parameters (long parameter list) to the extracted method, it becomes stinky.

Instead of creating temporary objects from a concrete object, keep the object and pass that to the extracted method:

```
public String addConnection(String firstName, String prefix,
        String middleName, String lastName, Date z,
        ConnectionType connectionType);
```

The preceding code can be refactored using a new request object, call it `PersonName`. Move `firstName`, `lastName`, and so on to this new class. Add getters/setters for these attributes and pass this to the `addConnection` method. Also change the `buildName()` method to accept the `PersonName` object:

```
public String addConnection(PersonName personName, Date z,
        ConnectionType connectionType);


protected String buildName(PersonName name) {
        StringBuilder personName = new StringBuilder();
        if (name.getPrefix() != null) {
           personName.append(name.getPrefix()).append(SPACE);
        }
        if (name.getFirstName() != null) {
           personName.append(name.getFirstName()).append(SPACE);
        }
        if (name.getMiddleName() != null) {

            personName.append(name.getMiddleName()).append(SPACE);
        }
        if (name.getLastName() != null) {
          personName.append(name.getLastName());
        }
        return personName.toString();
    }
```

Here, the request object holds all parameters as class members. So, if a new field is needed to pass to the method, just add a new attribute to the request class. If we need to pass the name suffix, we don't have to change the `addConenction` method.

Large classes (aka GOD object)

Like long methods, large classes are hard to maintain. It also violates the single responsibility principle. In other words, they are known as GOD objects. Like almighty GOD, doing everything.

Delegation is the best approach to handle this smell. S/W development teams have a manager, database administrators, architects, UI designers, developers, testers, and so on, and everybody plays a role. So, is it possible to have one member doing everything?

Similarly, a single class cannot do everything; it increases complexity and reduces extensibility. Large classes should delegate responsibilities to other members.

Following is an example where `TourConductor` is a class responsible for conducting tours. It has many responsibilities such as ticket booking, local cab/ bus booking, hotel booking, marketing, providing food to the guests, noting down expenses, keeping the account up-to-date, and so on. Instead of a single class doing all, refactoring and delegating responsibilities to many classes can set the `TourConductor` free.

Following is the class diagram of `TourConductor`:

Agent classes

We often see classes calling a series of methods on another class to perform logic. These classes are called agents; better if we can bypass them. Instead of an agent invoking the methods of another class, the latter class should provide a method for the client.

Remember the `buildName` example?

Look at the `PersonName` class and the `buildName()` method that builds the name from inputs:

```
public class PersonName implements Serializable {

    private static final long serialVersionUID = 1L;
    private String firstName;
    private String middleName;
    private String lastName;
    ...
    All getters and setters
}

protected String buildName(PersonName name) {
        StringBuilder personName = new StringBuilder();
        if (name.getPrefix() != null) {
           personName.append(name.getPrefix()).append(SPACE);
        }
        if (name.getFirstName() != null) {
           personName.append(name.getFirstName()).append(SPACE);
        }
        if (name.getMiddleName() != null) {

            personName.append(name.getMiddleName()).append(SPACE);
        }
        if (name.getLastName() != null) {
          personName.append(name.getLastName());
        }
        return personName.toString();
}
```

Here, `OnceYouBuyYouStartCryingTelephone` is an agent class. `PersonName` should provide a method to `getformattedName()` instead of another class accessing all fields of a `PersonName` class.

Move the method from the builder method to `PersonName` and then replace all calls to the builder method with `PersonName.getFormattedName();`.

Lazy, dead classes and dead code

Class inheritance creates many classes, which are inherited from a base class but never used or invoked at all. They are conceptually dead classes.

Often we refactor agent classes but don't delete them. They are no longer referred to and, hence, should be removed. It violates the YAGNI principle—You Ain't Gonna Need It.

The `buildName()` method in the `OnceYouBuyYouStartCryingTelephone` class is dead once we move the method to the `PersonName` class.

We create methods for future use but no one calls these. These methods are dead code. They create ambiguity. Readers, don't understand what to do? Method stays forever and creates more confusion?

Many eclipse plugins help to find out dead code/class. CodePro™ is one of them. The following screenshot shows the CodePro dead code finder in Eclipse:

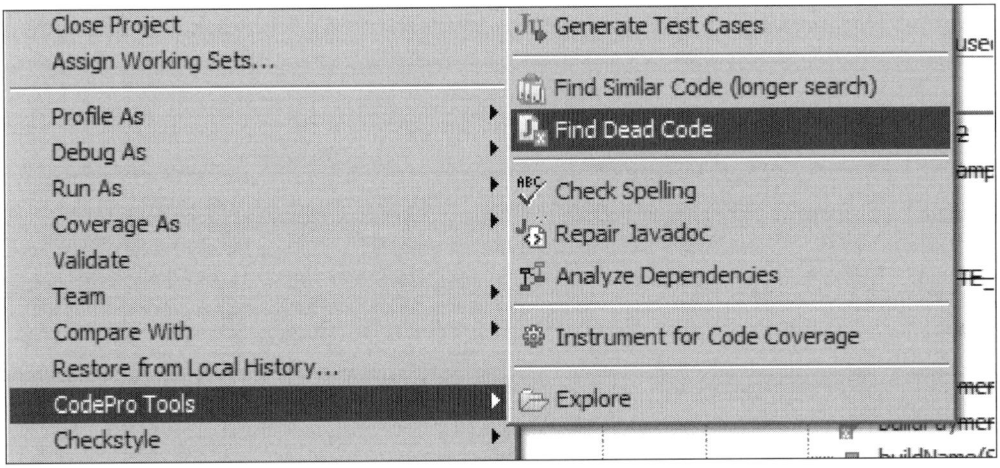

We can see the result of dead code search using CodePro in the following screenshot:

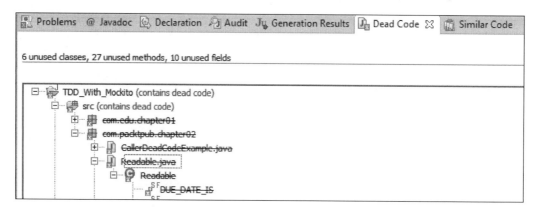

Over engineering (speculative generality)

S/W engineers speculate and over-engineer. When we develop, we think of special conditions for the future, create hooks, and increase the complexity of the system. It defeats the YAGNI principle.

I was helping a developer with a performance issue, who was working with a feature to display a list of items in a disclosure panel (blinds), where each row is expandable. Headers display a minimal set of data and when the user clicks on the header, the blind is expanded to display details.

Many UI frameworks provide this facility. For better performance, you should load only the header information and when the user clicks on the header, system should fetch the detail data.

The developer thought of a future enhancement that the layout of the detail section of each blind may not be the same; depending upon data, layout may be changed. He coded a layout manager to handle this future requirement. But this requirement never came; it defeated the main purpose of lazy loading. Rather, it increased the complexity.

Wrong inheritance (refused bequest)

Inheritance is a good thing to do, but often we create a hierarchy of classes, where seldom a class belongs to the ladder. This subclass has only few things in common with the superclass, but mainly works with its own set of features.

To refactor, use delegation. Instead of inheriting from the superclass, create a superclass instance and delegate calls to that instance.

Summary

This chapter covered refactoring and code smell. It defined refactoring and provided information about the refactoring schedule, the rationale behind refactoring, and when to trigger or stop refactoring. This chapter elaborated on code smell and provided simple examples to understand the refactoring and code smell concepts.

With this chapter, the reader should be able to identify and refactor code smells.

Chapter 3, *Applying TDD*, explains the life cycle of Test-Driven Development (TDD) and focuses on getting the reader quickly started with it.

3
Applying TDD

The previous chapters, *Chapter 1*, *Getting Familiar with TDD* and *Chapter 2*, *Refactoring – Roll the Dice*, gave us an overview of TDD, refactoring, and code smells from 1000 feet. It's time to take a closer look.

Now we know that the automated unit tests are a safety net for refactoring. Unit tests are re-run with every code change; failing tests indicate that something went wrong. So, the code is monitored continuously.

In this chapter we will apply Test-Driven Development (TDD) to write testfirst code.

Understanding different test types

We write tests for anything that can break basically into an algorithm or a logic, for example, the logic of calculating service tax. But we don't write tests for obvious things that can't go wrong, such as getters/setters of data transfer objects or constructors or any class that just sets the value from one object to another object (doesn't perform any conversion). But for data transfer objects, if I add a special logic for `hashCode()` or `equals()` methods, I should definitely write tests to validate the logic.

Test-Driven Development (TDD) is the new way of programming. Here the rule is very simple; it is as follows:

1. Write a test to add a new capability (automate tests).
2. Write code only to satisfy tests.
3. Re-run the tests—if any test is broken, revert the change.

4. Refactor and make sure all tests are green.

5. Continue with step 1.

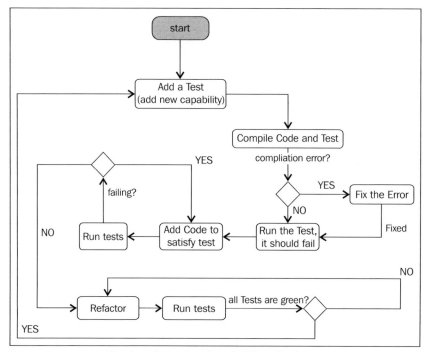

The given figure describes the life cycle of TDD

Have you ever faced a situation where you added new capabilities to a module and found that these new capabilities broke the existing functionalities and you had to rework every bit of code you added?

As shown in the following picture, the left-hand side represents functionalities before enhancement:

Before   **After**

Functionality is broken after enhancement

 This can happen if this rule of thumb is not followed — *Do not write any code unless you have a failing unit test and do not write more code than is sufficient to make the test pass.* Big upfront coding creates this issue.

Test-Driven Development reduces the time to market. From the starting, small testable pieces are developed; testers can test and accept the features from the very beginning instead of waiting for the end of development.

The following figure represents the old way of software development, the horizontal axis is time and the vertical axis is features. Here, features start moving after the testing has started. So, time to market a feature is dependent on all steps—redesign, coding, and testing.

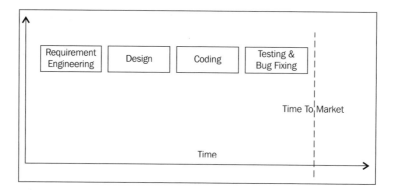

The following figure shows the TDD life cycle. This is iterative in nature. Here coding and testing starts very early. Features are delivered to customers faster than the previous way. First, requirement elicitation is conducted; as soon as the key requirements are gathered the design phase starts. Once the base line architecture is complete, the coding starts. Finally, once the testable unit is coded, the testing phase starts. So, the deliverable feature is ready as soon as the testing of the first testable unit is done.

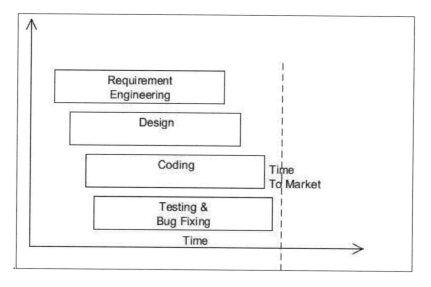

Understanding TDD – a real-life example

We will apply TDD for a healthcare domain problem.

Definition

Design a healthcare system for an imaginary health service provider **Q2HS** (**Quickest Quality Health Service**). Q2HS is new to healthcare and doesn't have tie-ups with any insurance company. They need a system to generate bills and receive money from patients. The bill will include patients' account numbers, procedure details, and charges. The system should support all available payment options.

Common healthcare vocabulary

Different languages/words create ambiguity and confusion. So, if we have a common vocabulary that everyone understands, it gives clarity.

Also, proper naming doesn't need any documentation. Metaphors or commonly-used names for classes/methods make it simple to understand the intent of the code.

Like other domains, healthcare has its own vocabulary.

Procedure

The services provided to a patient, for example, physiotherapy, injection, oxygen, and so on. Each procedure has a unique code.

The service catalogue

The cost of procedure changes with time. Service catalogues keep track of price for each procedure/service. Systems should allow users to update costs of services and allow configuring procedures.

MRN

To uniquely identify patients, we need to generate a Medical Record Number (MRN) system.

Encounter

It's a contract between a hospital and a patient, an encounter is created when a patient is admitted to a hospital. Encounter has start and discharge date and time, guarantor information, insurance details, and so on. Multiple visits to a hospital creates multiple encounters.

Unless procedure setup is ready, it cannot be used. First create a procedure and add it to the service catalogue.

Create a test class and add a test to add a procedure to the catalogue.

A procedure needs an ID and service description. In the test method type `Procedure` and pass the ID and description to it. Compiler will raise an error saying that the `Procedure` class doesn't exist. Create a class called `Procedure`:

```
ServiceCatalogueTest.java

package com.packtpub.chapter03;

import org.junit.Test;

public class ServiceCatalogueTest {

    @Test
    public void user_can_add_a_service_to_catalogue() {
        Procedure proc = new Procedure("1234", "Basic Oxygen Setup");

    }
}
```

Create a catalogue object and pass a `Procedure` object to it. Resolve all compilation errors, create new classes, and add the required methods:

```
public void user_can_add_a_service_to_catalogue() {
    Procedure proc = new Procedure("1234", "Basic Oxygen Setup");
    ServiceCatalogue catalogue = new ServiceCatalogue();

    catalogue.add(proc, BigDecimal.TEN);
    assertNotNull(catalogue.find(proc.getId()));
    assertEquals(catalogue.find(proc.getId()), proc);
}
```

The system will generate a class with empty `add()` and `find()` methods.

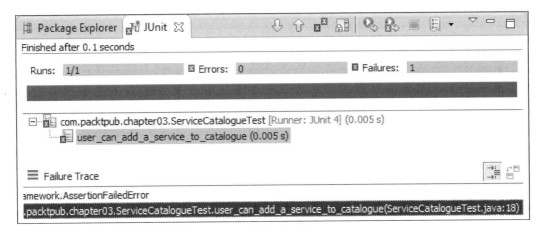

Now run the test. The test will fail since it expects a procedure, but the `find()` method returns `null`.

Now write a code to pass the test. Return a procedure from the `find()` method.

```java
public Procedure find(String id) {
    return new Procedure(null, null);
}
```

Re-run the test. Oops! It is still failing, it is expecting the procedure that was passed to the add() method. Following is the stacktrace of the error:

java.lang.AssertionError: expected:<com.packtpub.chapter03.Procedure@1a16869> but was:<com.packtpub.chapter03.Procedure@1cde100>

Add code to store the Procedure class that was passed to add() and return it from find():

```java
public class ServiceCatalogue {
    private Procedure proc;
    public void add(Procedure proc, BigDecimal ten) {
        this.proc = proc;
    }
    public Object find(String id) {
        return proc;
    }
}
```

Run the test again.

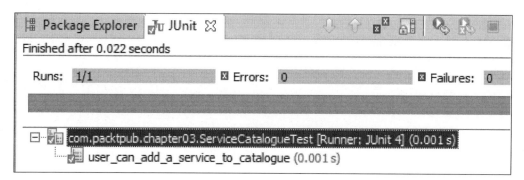

Voila! The first green bar. Test passed!!!

Time to add a new capability to the catalogue. The find() method returns the procedure that was added, but it shouldn't return any procedure if the procedure is not configured.

Add a test to validate that:

```java
@Test
public void catalogue_returns_null_for_an_unconfigured_procedure_id()
throws Exception {
    Procedure proc = new Procedure("1234", "Basic Oxygen Setup");
    ServiceCatalogue catalogue = new ServiceCatalogue();
    catalogue.add(proc, BigDecimal.TEN);
```

```
    assertNull(catalogue.find("4567"));
}
```

Run the test. The test is failing with the following error **java.lang.AssertionError: expected null**, but was <com.packtpub.chapter03.Procedure@1a16869>.

Add code to pass the test. Okay, we will return the procedure if the ID matches:

```
public Procedure find(String id) {
    if (proc.getId().equals(id)) {
        return proc;
    }
    return null;
}
```

Re-run the test. Yes green again!

We should add a new capability now. Does it work for multiple procedures?

```
@Test
public void catalogue_returns_procedure_for_a_configured_procedure_
id() {
    Procedure proc1 = new Procedure("1234", "Basic Oxygen Setup");
    Procedure proc2 = new Procedure("6789", "Basic Oxygen Setup");
    ServiceCatalogue catalogue = new ServiceCatalogue();
        catalogue.add(proc1, BigDecimal.TEN);
    catalogue.add(proc2, BigDecimal.TEN);
    assertNotNull("Expected a procedure",catalogue.find("1234"));
}
```

Nope! The new test is failing. It expects the proc1 object but gets nothing. Okay, the problem is we store only the latest object that we passed to the add() method. We should keep all procedures. To do this, use a container to store all procedures and look up the container to find the procedure by ID.

What should we use as a container? Array? Vector? List?

Arrays cannot grow automatically; we don't have any synchronization issue, so let's use an ArrayList object:

```
public class ServiceCatalogue {
    private List<Procedure> procs = new ArrayList<Procedure>();

    public void add(Procedure proc, BigDecimal ten) {
        procs.add(proc);
    }
```

```
public Procedure find(String id) {
    for (Procedure proc : procs) {
        if (proc.getId().equals(id)) {
            return proc;
        }
    }
    return null;
}
```

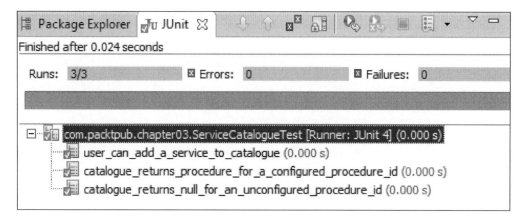

Wait a minute. A catalogue should return the price of a procedure. The `ServiceCatalogue` class should provide an API to return the price. So, add a test to query price. We can use existing tests for this, just need to change the name. Add a method named `BigDecimal findPriceBy(String id)` to `ServiceCatalogue` to resolve the compilation error:

```
public void catalogue_returns_procedure_and_price_for_a_configured_
procedure() {
//ignoring code for space
assertEquals(catalogue.findPriceBy(proc1.getId()), BigDecimal.TEN);
assertEquals(catalogue.findPriceBy(proc2.getId()), BigDecimal.ONE);
}
```

Add code to `findPriceBy(String id)` to pass the test. Store the price in a variable.

No, the test is failing for the first procedure. It returns ONE but test expects TEN. Same issue is that we are storing the price in a variable but we need to store all procedure prices.

We need a data structure to store the procedure ID and its price.

Change the code to pass the failing test. Keep a map of the ID and price. Return the price from the map:

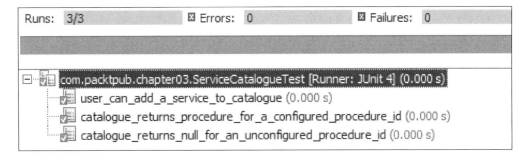

Yes, all green again!

Now, it is time to refactor the tests. A duplicate code is present in the test class. Each test method is creating instances of ServiceCatalogue.

JUnit provides an annotation @Before. If this annotation is added to a public method, that method is invoked before every test. This is equivalent to the setUp() method of JUnit 3.X.

Similarly, there is the @After annotation. This annotation acts as the teardown() method. After every test, teardown() is called.

Create a public method setUp() or init(), add @Before annotation, and create an instance of ServiceCatalogue in this method. From all tests, remove the initialization constructor call.

Re-run the tests to make sure that everything is working fine:

```java
public class ServiceCatalogueTest {
  ServiceCatalogue catalogue;
    @Before public void setup() {
      catalogue = new ServiceCatalogue();
    }

    @Test
    public void user_can_add_a_service_to_catalogue() {
        Procedure proc = new Procedure("1234", "Basic Oxygen Setup");
        catalogue.add(proc, BigDecimal.TEN);
        assertNotNull(catalogue.find(proc.getId()));
        assertEquals(catalogue.find(proc.getId()), proc);
    }
```

Similarly, a duplicate code is present. We are constructing a procedure object and setting it to the catalogue. Create a **Plain Old Java Object (POJO)** class that accepts the ID, description, and price, add a method in the test class to accept variable arguments of that POJO class, and set the procedure to the catalogue:

```
private void addToCatalogue(Proc... procs) {
    for (Proc proc : procs) {
      catalogue.add(proc.procedure, proc.price);
    }
}
```

```
From tests, call this method:
addToCatalogue(new Proc("1234", "Injection", BigDecimal.TEN),
        new Proc("5678", "Basic Oxygen Setup", BigDecimal.ONE));
```

We are done with refactoring; a new functionality can be started. Follow the TDD flowchart and add a new capability.

Summary

In this chapter we learned what type of tests should be written, the life cycle of TDD, steps to apply TDD, and how to apply TDD in a real-life projects.

In the next chapter we will explore the two types of TDD—inside-out and outside-in.

4
Understanding the Difference between Inside-out and Outside-in

In this chapter, we will cover different styles of TDD and write code using them.

Commonly, TDD has the following styles:

- Outside-in
- Inside-out

Understanding outside-in

Generally, the outside-in approach covers use case level functionality or is intended for acceptance tests. These tests provide regression suits and system documentation; if they fail, user/customer acceptance also fails.

In this category, developers pick a story or use case and drill into low-level unit tests. Basically, the objective is to obtain high-level design. The different system interfaces are identified and abstracted. Once different layers/interfaces are identified, unit-level coding can be started.

Here, developers look at the system boundary and create a boundary interface depending upon a use case/story. Then, collaborating classes are created. Mock objects can act as a collaborating class. This approach of development relies on code for abstraction.

Acceptance Test-Driven Development (ATDD) falls into this category. FitNesse fixtures provide support for ATDD. This is stateful. It is also known as the top-down approach.

An example of ATDD

As a health professional (doctor), I should get the health information of all my critical patients who are admitted as soon as I'm around 100 ft from the hospital.

Here, how patient information is periodically stored in the server, how GPS tracks the doctor, how the system registers the doctor's communication medium (sends report to the doctor by e-mail or text), and so on can be mocked out. A test will be conducted to deal with how to fetch patient data for a doctor and send the report quickly. Gradually, other components will be coded.

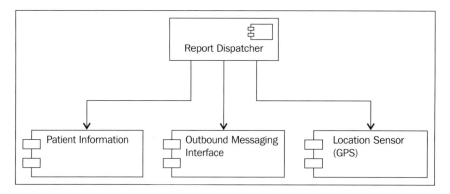

The preceding figure represents the high-level components of the user story.

Here, **Report Dispatcher** is notified when a doctor approaches a hospital, then the dispatcher fetches patient information for the doctor and sends him the patient record. **Patient Information**, **Outbound Messaging Interface**, and **Location Sensor (GPS)** parts are mocked, and the dispatcher acts as a collaborator.

In *Chapter 1, Getting Familiar with TDD*, the `TaxCalculator` example, we passed taxable income as the input and got payable tax as the output. Now we have a requirement to calculate the taxable income from the total income, calculate the payable tax, and send an e-mail to the client with details.

We have to gather the annual income, medical expense, house loan premium, life insurance details, provident fund deposit, and apply the following rule to calculate the taxable income:

- Up to USD 100,000 is not taxable and can be invested as medical insurance, provident fund, or house loan principal payment
- Up to USD 150,000 can be used as house rent or house loan interest

Now we will build a `TaxConsultant` application using the outside-in style.

Following are the steps:

1. Create a new test class `com.packtpub.chapter04.outside.in.TaxConsultantTest` under the `test` source folder.

2. We need to perform three tasks; that are, calculate the taxable income, the payable tax, and send an e-mail to a client. We will create a class `TaxConsultant` to perform these tasks. We will be using Mockito to mock out external behavior. Add a test to check that when a client has investment, then our consultant deducts an amount from the total income and calculates the taxable income. Add a test `when_deductable_present_then_taxable_income_is_less_than_the_total_income ()` to verify it so that it can calculate the taxable income:

```
@Test
public void when_deductable_present_then_taxable_income_
is_less_than_the_total_income () {
  TaxConsultant consultant = new TaxConsultant();
}
```

Add the class under the `src` source folder. Now we have to pass different amounts to the consultant. Create a method `consult()` and pass the following values:

```
@Test
public void when_deductable_present_then_taxable_income_is_less_
than_the_total_income () {
  TaxConsultant consultant = new TaxConsultant();
  double totalIncome = 1200000;
  double homeLoanInterest = 150000;
  double homeLoanPrincipal   =20000;
  double providentFundSavings = 50000;
  double lifeInsurancePremium = 30000;

  consultant.consult(totalIncome,homeLoanInterest,
homeLoanPrincipal,providentFundSavings,
lifeInsurancePremium);
}
```

In the outside-in approach, we mock out objects with interesting behavior. We will mock out taxable income behavior and create an interface named `TaxbleIncomeCalculator`. This interface will have a method to calculate the taxable income. We read that a long parameter list is code smell; we will refactor it later:

```
public interface TaxbleIncomeCalculator {
    double calculate(double totalIncome, double homeLoanInterest,
    double homeLoanPrincipal, double providentFundSavings, double
    lifeInsurancePremium);
}
```

3. Pass this interface to `TaxConsultant` as the constructor argument:

```
@Test
public void when_deductable_present_then_taxable_income_is_less_
than_the_total_income () {
    TaxbleIncomeCalculator taxableIncomeCalculator = null;
    TaxConsultant consultant = new TaxConsultant
                            (taxableIncomeCalculator);
```

We need a tax calculator to verify that behavior. Create an interface called `TaxCalculator`:

```
public interface TaxCalculator {
    double calculate(double taxableIncome);
}
```

4. Pass this interface to `TaxConsultant`:

```
TaxConsultant consultant = new TaxConsultant(taxableIncomeCalculat
or,taxCalculator);
```

Now, time to verify the collaboration. We will use Mockito to create mock objects from the interfaces. We will learn more about mocking using Mockito in *Chapter 6, Mockito Magic*. For now, the `@Mock` annotation creates a proxy mock object. In the `setUp` method, we will use `MockitoAnnotations.initMocks(this);` to create the objects:

```
@Mock TaxbleIncomeCalculator taxableIncomeCalculator;
@Mock TaxCalculator taxCalculator;

TaxConsultant consultant;
@Before
public void setUp() {
    MockitoAnnotations.initMocks(this);
    consultant= new TaxConsultant(
        taxableIncomeCalculator,taxCalculator);
}
```

5. Now in `test`, verify that the `consultant` class calls `TaxableIncomeCalculator` and `TaxableIncomeCalculator` makes a call to

6. `TaxCalculator`. Mockito has the `verify` method to test that:

```
verify(taxableIncomeCalculator, only())
calculate(eq(totalIncome), eq(homeLoanInterest),
eq(homeLoanPrincipal), eq(providentFundSavings),
eq(lifeInsurancePremium));

verify(taxCalculator,only()).calculate(anyDouble());
```

Here, we are verifying that the `consultant` class delegates the call to mock objects. `only()` checks that the method was called at least once on the mock object. `eq()` checks that the value passed to the mock object's method is equal to some value.

Here, the test will fail since we don't have the calls. We will add the following code to pass the test:

```
public class TaxConsultant {

  private final TaxbleIncomeCalculator taxbleIncomeCalculator;
  private final TaxCalculator calculator;

  public TaxConsultant(TaxbleIncomeCalculator
    taxableIncomeCalculator, TaxCalculator calc) {
    this.taxbleIncomeCalculator =
      taxableIncomeCalculator;
    this.calculator = calc;
  }

  public void consult(double totalIncome, double homeLoanInterest,
double homeLoanPrincipal, double providentFundSavings, double
lifeInsurancePremium) {

    double taxableIncome = taxbleIncomeCalculator.calculate
      (totalIncome,homeLoanInterest, homeLoanPrincipal,
        providentFundSavings,lifeInsurancePremium);

    double payableTax= calculator.calculate(taxableIncome);
  }

}
```

The test is being passed; we can now add another delegator for e-mail and call it `EmailSender`.

7. Our façade class is ready. Now we need to use TDD for each interface we extracted. We have already done this in the `TaxCalculator` example in *Chapter 1, Getting Familiar with TDD*. Similarly, we can apply TDD for `TaxableIncomeCalculator` and `EmailSender`.

Understanding the advantages and disadvantages of outside-in

The advantages are as follows:

- Outside-in is an acceptance test or customer oriented
- System interfaces are not predefined; tests identify the interfaces and protocol of interaction
- Design evolves from the test

The disadvantages are as follows:

- Maintainability of tests.
- If use case or story criteria changes, it creates a ripple effect in unit-level codes, which is a single place of failure.
- Production code lives with mocks and fakes. If forgotten, they live forever.

Understanding inside-out

Inside-out is the form that is mostly followed by developers. High-level objects and interaction are designed first, then unit level classes are coded using TDD. Mostly inside-out is a stateless development. Pure JUnit tests with mocking fall under this section.

Developers start with a component/class and add tests for the component; as the tests evolve, new components and interaction between these new components come into picture.

This is also known as the bottom-up approach. Inside-out is used once the outside-in interfaces are coded. This approach is also known as classical TDD.

The following figure describes the classical approach of the Report Dispatcher example:

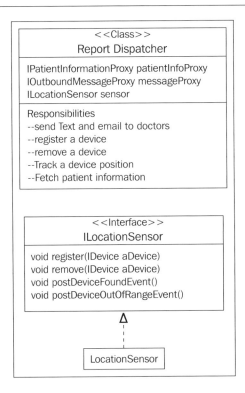

The `ReportDisptacher` class and its collaborators are defined when the architecture is designed..

All methods such as `register()` and `postDeviceFoundEvent()` are defined when the baseline architecture is designed.

Using TDD, the actual implementation class `LocationSensor` can be coded.

For the tax calculation example, we will first start with three interfaces. Using TDD, we will unit test them and create the façade class using these three interfaces.

Understanding the advantages and disadvantages of inside-out

The advantages are as follows:

- Maintainable, clean production code

The disadvantages are as follows:

- Upfront design is already done.
- Time to market a feature is slow as compared to outside-in because someone is creating the big upfront design. Unless the layers are created, unit-level tests cannot be started.

Summary

This chapter provided an overview of classical and mockist TDD. In classical TDD, real objects are used and integrated, and mocks are only preferred if a real object is not easy to instantiate. In mockist TDD, mocks have higher priority than real objects.

More about classical and mockist TDD can be found at `http://martinfowler.com`.

In the next chapter, we will cover test double. Mock objects are a special type of test double.

5
Test Doubles

We know about stunt doubles—a trained replacement used for dangerous action sequences in movies, like jumping out of the Empire State Building, a fight sequence on top of a burning train, jumping from an airplane, or similar actions, mainly fight scenes. Stunt doubles are used to protect the elite real actors or when the actor is not available.

Similarly, sometimes it is not possible to unit test a code because of the unavailability of collaborator objects or the cost of instantiation for the collaborator.

If a code is dependent on database access, it is not possible to unit test the code unless the database is available, or if my code needs to send information to a printer and my machine is not connected to LAN.

Test doubles act as stunt doubles. They are a skilled replacement of the `collaborator` class.

Test doubles can be created to impersonate collaborators.

Categories of test doubles

Test doubles are categorized into four types. The following figure demonstrates the types:

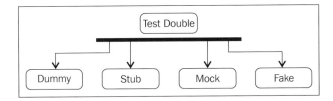

Dummy

An example of a dummy would be a movie scene where the double doesn't perform anything, but only its screen presence is required. It is used when the actual actor is not present but his attendance is needed for a scene, for example, watching the US open tennis finals match.

Similarly, dummy objects are passed for mandatory parameter objects:

```
Book javaBook = new Book("Java 101", "123456");
Member dummyMember = new DummyMember());
javaBook.issueTo(dummyMember);
assertEquals(javaBook.numberOfTimesIssued(),1);
```

Here, a dummy member was created and passed to a book object in order to test if that book can report how many times it was issued. Here, a member is not used anywhere, but is needed for `Book.issueTo(...)`.

Stub

A stub delivers indirect inputs to the caller when the stub's methods are called. Stubs are programmed only for the test scope. Stubs may record other information, such as how many times they are invoked.

Account transaction should be rolled back if the ATM money dispenser fails to dispense money. How can we test this when we don't have the ATM machine, or how can we simulate the scenario in which the dispenser fails:

```
public interface Dispenser {
  void dispense(BigDecimal amount) throws DispenserFailed;
}

public class AlwaysFailingDispenserStub implements Dispenser{
  public void dispense(BigDecimal amount) throws DispenserFailed{
    throw new DispenseFiled (ErrorType.HARDWARE,"not responding");
  }
}

class ATMTest...
@Test
public void transaction_is_rolledback_when_hardware_fails() {
  Account myAccount = new Account("John", 2000.00);
  TransactionManager txMgr =
    TransactionManager.forAccount(myAccount);
  txMgr.registerMoneyDispenser(new AlwaysFailingDispenserStub());
```

```
    WithdrawalResponse response = txMgr.withdraw(500.00);
    assertEquals(false, response.wasSuccess());
    assertEquals(2000.00, myAccount.remainingAmount());
  }
```

Here, `AlwaysFailingDispenserStub` raises an error whenever the `dispense()` method is invoked. It allows testing of the transactional behavior when hardware is not present.

Fake

Fake objects are working implementations; the class mostly extends the original class, but usually performs a hack, which makes it unsuitable for production.

```
public class AddressDao extends SimpleJdbcDaoSupport{
  public void batchInsertOrUpdate(List<AddressDTO> addressList,
    User user){
    List<AddressDTO> insertList =
      buildListWhereLastChangeTimeMissing(addressList);
    List<AddressDTO> updateList =
      buildListWhereLastChangeTimeValued(addressList);
    int rowCount =   0;
    if (!insertList.isEmpty()) {
      rowCount =
        getSimpleJdbcTemplate().batchUpdate(INSERT_SQL,…);
    }
    if(!updateList.isEmpty()){
      rowCount +=
        getSimpleJdbcTemplate().batchUpdate(UPDATE_SQL,…);
    }
    if(addressList.size() != rowCount){
      raiseErrorForDataInconsistency(…);
    }
  }
}
```

`AddressDAO` extends from the Spring framework class and provides an API to mass update. The same method is used to create a new address and update the existing; if the count doesn't match, it raises an error. This class cannot be tested directly; it needs `getSimpleJdbcTemplate()`.

```
public class FakeAddressDao extends AddressDao{
  public SimpleJdbcTemplate getSimpleJdbcTemplate() {
    return jdbcTemplate;
  }
}
```

FakeAddressDao extends from AddressDao but only overrides the getSimpleJdbcTemplate() method and returns a JDBC template stub. So this class cannot be used in production, but inherits all functionalities of the DAO, so this can be used for testing.

Mock

Mock objects have expectations; a test expects a value from a mock object, and during execution, the mock object returns the expected result. Also, mock objects can keep track of invocation count, that is, how many times a method is called on a mock object.

```
public class ATMTest {

  @Mock Dispenser failingDispenser;
  @Before
  public void setUp() throws Exception {
    MockitoAnnotations.initMocks(this);
  }

  @Test
  public void transaction_is_rolledback_when_hardware_fails()
    throws DispenserFailed {
    Account myAccount = new Account(2000.00, "John");
    TransactionManager txMgr =
      TransactionManager.forAccount(myAccount);
    txMgr.registerMoneyDispenser(failingDispenser);

    doThrow(new
      DispenserFailed()).when(failingDispenser).
        dispense(isA(BigDecimal.class));
    txMgr.withdraw(500);
    assertTrue(2000.00 == myAccount.getRemianingBalance());
    verify(failingDispenser, new
      Times(1)).dispense(isA(BigDecimal.class));

  }

}
```

Here, the mock (Mockito) version of the ATM test is used. The same object can be used in different tests, just the expectation needs to be set. Here, doThrow() raises an error whenever the mock object is called with any BigDecimal value.

Summary

This chapter provided an overview of test doubles and different test double types with examples, including topics such as dummy, stub, mock, and fake.

In the next chapter, we will cover Mockito. It will explain the concept of mock objects using the Mockito framework and provide examples to understand the Mockito APIs.

6
Mockito Magic

This chapter distills the Mockito framework to its main core and provides technical examples. No previous knowledge of mocking is necessary.

The following topics are covered in this chapter:

- Overview of Mockito
- Qualities of unit tests
- Exploring Mockito APIs
- Examples of using of Mockito

An overview of Mockito

Mockito is an open source mock unit testing framework for Java. In the previous chapter we read about test doubles and mock objects. Mockito allows mock object creation, verification, and stubbing.

To know more about Mockito, visit the following link:

```
http://code.google.com/p/mockito/
```

Why you should use Mockito

Automated tests are a safety net, they run and notify if the system is broken so that the offending code can be fixed very quickly.

If a test suite runs for an hour, the purpose of quick feedback is compromised.

Every time a piece of code is checked-in, the automated tests run and take hours to complete. So, a developer cannot check in new code until the test run is complete. This blocks the progress of the development.

A test may take time to execute due to the following reasons:

- Maybe a test acquires a connection from the database and fetches/updates data
- Connects to the Internet and downloads files
- Interacts with an SMTP server to send e-mail
- Performs I/O operations

Now the question comes, *do we really need to acquire a database connection or download files to unit test code?*

The answer is yes. If it doesn't connect to a database or download the latest stock price, few parts of the system remains untested. So, DB interaction or network connection is mandatory for a few parts of the system. To unit test these parts, the external dependencies need to be mocked out.

Mockito plays a key role to mock out external dependencies. It mocks out database connection or any external I/O behavior so that the actual logic can be unit tested.

Qualities of unit testing

Unit tests should adhere to the following rules:

- **Order independent and isolated**: The test class ATest.java should not be dependent on the output of the test class BTest.java, or the test shouldn't fail if BTest.java is executed after ATest.java
- **Trouble-free setup and run**: Unit tests should not require DB connection or Internet connection or clean up temp directory
- **Effortless execution**: Unit tests should not be "It works fine on Server abc but doesn't run on my local"
- **Formula 1 execution**: A test should not take more than a second to finish the execution

Here, Mockito plays a key role; it provides APIs to mock out the external dependencies and achieve the qualities mentioned here.

Drinking Mockito

Download the latest Mockito binary from the following link and add to the project dependency:

```
http://code.google.com/p/mockito/downloads/list
```

To add Mockito JAR files to the project dependency, carry out the following steps:

1. Extract the JAR files into a folder.

2. Open an Eclipse project.

3. Go to the **Libraries** tab in the project build path.

4. Click on the **Add External JARs...** button and browse to the Mockito JAR folder.

5. Select all JAR files and hit **OK**.

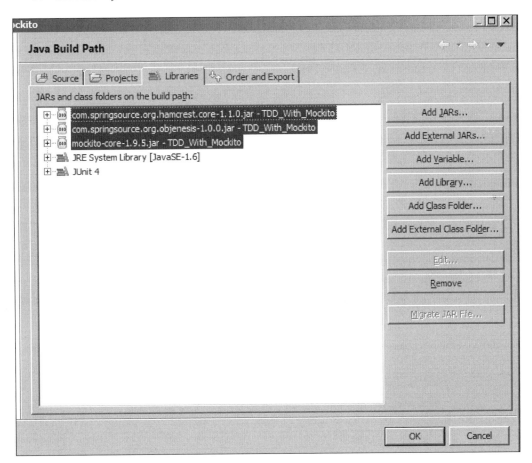

Retail shops publicize different promotional offers such as "buy one get 2 free" or "buy 2.5 kg sugar and get 30 percent off". The following `BiggestBazarRetail` class represents a retail shop:

```
public class BiggestBazarRetail {

  public int issueDiscountForItemsExpireIn30Days(double discountRate) {
   List<Item> headingExpiryItems = inventory.getItemsExpireInAMonth();
     for (Item anItem : headingExpiryItems) {
        double newPrice = anItem.getPrice() - anItem.getPrice() *
   discountRate;
        if (newPrice > anItem.getBasePrice()) {
           inventory.update(anItem, newPrice);
           publicAddressSystem.announce(new Offer(anItem, newPrice));
        }
     }
   return inventory.itemsUpdated();
}
     public BiggestBazarRetail(Inventory inventory,
           PublicAddressSystem publicAddressSystem) {}
}
```

The preceding `BiggestBazarRetail` class issues discounts on items. It fetches all items that are going to expire, applies the discount if the new price is not less than the base price, and then updates the item price and announces the new price in the public address system.

We need to unit test the `discount()` method.

In order to execute the `discount()` method, the `Inventory` and `PublicAddressSystem` (PAS) objects are required. They are resource-intensive objects — `Inventory` accesses databases and instantiates if PAS requires hardware, driver software, and so on.

We will use Mockito to mock these two objects.

 Mockito cannot mock final classes, methods, anonymous classes, and primitive types.

Mockito provides static methods for mocking any class. We need to import the static `mock()` method. Then, to create the mock object, we just need to pass the class type. The following screenshot shows the details:

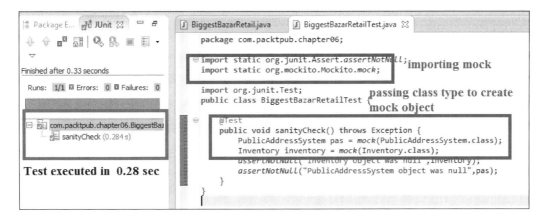

Change the `Inventory` class to a final class and run the test.

The following screenshot shows that the test will fail because the `Inventory` class is a final class:

Annotation is also supported for mocking.

Annotate a variable definition with `@Mock` and in the setup method (any method that runs before every test — JUnit 4.0 `@before`) call `MockitoAnnotation.initMocks(object)`.

The following screenshot describes the setup process:

```
import org.mockito.Mock;
import org.mockito.MockitoAnnotations;
public class BiggestBazarRetailTest {
   @Mock PublicAddressSystem pas;
   @Mock Inventory inventory;

   @Before
   public void setUp() {
     MockitoAnnotations.initMocks(this);
   }

   @Test
   public void mockAnnotation_creates_mock() throws Exception {
      assertNotNull("@Mock could not create inventory",inventory);
      assertNotNull("@Mock could not create  PublicAddressSystem " ,pas);
   }
```

Let's test the discount example. Carry out the following steps:

1. Create mock objects for `Inventory` and PAS.
2. Instantiate the test class and pass the mock objects as constructor arguments.
3. Add a test method and stub the mock objects to get the expected result.
4. Call the `issueDiscountForItemsExpiresIn30Days()` method.
5. Verify that the mock objects are invoked.

The code snippet shown in the following screenshot describes the details:

```java
stBazarRetail.java        J BiggestBazarRetailTest.java  ⊠
@Before
public void setUp() {
    MockitoAnnotations.initMocks(this);
    // Setup with mock objects
    bazar = new BiggestBazarRetail(inventory, pas);
}

@Test
public void issues_discount() throws Exception {
    // Creating expected item list
    Item soap = new Item("123", "Luxury Soap", 100.00, 50.00);
    expiredList.add(soap);

    // Stubbing database call for getItemsExpireInAMonth
    when(inventory.getItemsExpireInAMonth()).thenReturn(expiredList);
    // Stubbing update count
    when(inventory.itemsUpdated()).thenReturn(1);

    // Test
    bazar.issueDiscountForItemsExpireIn30Days(.30);

    //Verify that inventory update and public announcement were invoked
    verify(inventory).update(soap, 70.00);
    verify(pas).announce(isA(Offer.class));
}
```

Mockito provides `when-then` stubbing methods; `when()` is a static Mockito API method, we use it when we want the mock to return a particular value when a particular method is called.

Here, the first `bazar` object was created with two mock proxy objects; the database call was stubbed with returning a list of items. During execution, the Mockito proxy object returns this list whenever the `getItemsExpireInAMonth()` method is called.

The `verify()` method is a static method, which can be used to check the `void` methods and cover if a code execution path called this method or not.

In our example, `update(anItem, newPrice)` is a database update call. We don't have a database, so we had to pass the mock `inventory` object to stub the database call. If at least one item qualifies for discount, that item's price will be updated.

Hence, using `verify` we verified that our discount logic is working fine. How? We passed one item to the `discount()` method and it called an update on the inventory, which means that the object is qualified for discount. `verify` raises an error if the method on the mock object is not invoked but expected.

Now, we will pass an item which will not qualify for discount. The current item price is USD 100.00 and the base price was 90.00. Now if we issue a discount of 30 percent, the price will be 70.00, which is lower than the buying price. This will incur a loss; hence, no discount will be issued.

The following code snippet creates an `item` method with the base price USD 90.00 and current price USD 100.00:

```
@Test
public void when_no_item_qulifies_then_doesNOT_issue_discount() throws Exception {
    // Creating expected item list
    Item soap = new Item("123", "Luxury Soap", 100.00, 90.00);
    expiredList.add(soap);

    // Stubbing database call for getItemsExpireInAMonth
    when(inventory.getItemsExpireInAMonth()).thenReturn(expiredList);
    // Stubbing update count
    when(inventory.itemsUpdated()).thenReturn(1);

    // Test
    bazar.issueDiscountForItemsExpireIn30Days(.30);

    //Verify that inventory update and public announcement were invoked
    verify(inventory).update(isA(Item.class), anyDouble());
    verify(pas).announce(isA(Offer.class));
}
```

Run the test, it will fail saying that the inventory update was expected but not invoked.

Following is the failing test:

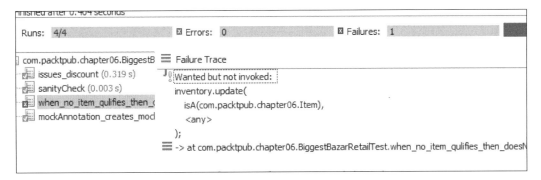

Verifying redundant invocation

To verify the redundant invocations, we need to go through the following:

Rationale

Mock objects are used to stub external dependencies. We set an expectation and a mock object returns the expected value. In some conditions a behavior should not be invoked, or sometimes we may need to call it a certain number of times. The `verify` method comes into the picture to verify the invocation of mock objects.

If a stubbed behavior should not be called but due to the bug in the code the method is called, verify if it flags the error. `Void` methods don't return values, `verify` is very handy to test a void method's behavior.

The `Verify()` method has an overloaded version which takes `Times` as an argument.

`Times` is a Mockito framework class of `org.mockito.internal.verification` and it takes an Integer argument `wantedNumberOfInvocations`.

If `0` is passed to `Times` it infers that the method will not be invoked in the testing path. We will pass `0` to `Times(0)` to make sure that the `update` and `announce` methods are not invoked. If a negative number is passed to the `Times` constructor, Mockito throws `MockitoException` - `org.mockito.exceptions.base.MockitoException`, and shows the **Negative value is not allowed here** error.

The following code snippet displays this:

```
        //Verify that NO inventory update and public announcement were invoked
        verify(inventory, new Times(0)).update(isA(Item.class), anyDouble());
        verify(pas,new Times(0)).announce(isA(Offer.class));
    }
```

Runs: 4/4   ☒ Errors: 0   ☒ Failures: 0

```
⊟ 🔲 com.packtpub.chapter06.BiggestBazarRetailTest [Runner: JUnit 4] (0.335 s)
    🔳 issues_discount (0.325 s)
    🔳 sanityCheck (0.004 s)
    🔳 when_no_item_qulifies_then_doesNOT_issue_discount (0.003 s)
    🔳 mockAnnotation_creates_mock (0.003 s)
```

Another way of checking that a method is never invoked is by using the `never()` method:

```
verify(inventory, never()).update(....);
```

The argument matcher

Argument matchers play a key role in mocking. Following are the rationale and examples of Argument matchers.

Rationale

Mock objects return expected values. But when it needs to return different values for different arguments, argument matcher comes into play. Suppose we have a method that takes a player name as the input and returns the number of runs as the output. We want to stub it and return 100 for `Sachin` and 10 for `xyz`. We have to use argument matcher to stub this.

Mockito returns expected values when a method is stubbed. If the method takes arguments, the argument must match during the execution. For example, the `getValue(int someValue)` method is stubbed in the following way:

```
when(mockObject.getValue(1)).thenReturn(expected value);
```

Here, the `getValue` method is called with `mockObject.getValue(100)`. Then, the parameter doesn't match (it is expected that the method will be called with 1, but at runtime it encounters 100), so the mock object fails to return the expected value. It will return the default value of the return type—if the return type is Boolean, it'll return false; if object then null, and so on.

Mockito verifies argument values in natural Java style by using an `equals()` method. Sometimes, we use argument matchers when extra flexibility is required.

Mockito provides built-in matchers such as `anyInt()`, `anyDouble()`, `anyString()`, `anyList()`, `anyCollection()`.

More built-in matchers and examples of custom argument matchers / hamcrest matchers can be found at the following link:

> http://docs.mockito.googlecode.com/hg/latest/org/mockito/Matchers. html

 Examples of other matchers are `isA(java.lang.Class<T> clazz)`, `any(java.lang.Class<T> clazz)`, and `eq(T)` or `eq(primitive value)`.

In the retail shop example, we verified invocation of announcement with `isA(Offer.class)`:

```
verify(pas).announce(isA(Offer.class));
```

`isA` checks that if the passed object is an instance of the class type passed in the `isA` argument. `any(T)` also works in the same way.

Why we need wildcard matchers

If a method creates a new object and invokes a method on a mock object, then from the test method we cannot control the input. In `publicAddressSystem. announce(new Offer(...));` it created a new offer and sent to the `announce` method. From the test we cannot get the that object.

> If we are using argument matchers, *all* arguments have to be provided by matchers.
>
> We're passing three arguments — all of them are passed using matchers:
>
> ```
> verify(mock).someMethod(anyInt(), anyString(),
> eq("third argument"));
> ```
>
> The following example will fail because the first and the third argument are not passed using matchers.
>
> ```
> verify(mock).someMethod(1, anyString(), "third
> argument");
> ```

The ArgumentMatcher class

The ArgumentMatcher class allows the creation of customized argument matchers. ArgumentMatcher is a hamcrest matcher with the predefined describeTo() method.

Use the Matchers.argThat(org.hamcrest.Matcher) method and pass an instance of the hamcrest matcher.

Consider a StockListener class, it takes a stock and then gets the quote from the stockbroker. If the current price is higher than the buying price, it sells the stock, otherwise it buys some more:

```
public class StockListener {
    private final StockBroker broker;

    public void takeAction(Stock stock){
        double currentPrice = broker.getQoute(stock);
        if(currentPrice <= stock.boughtAt()){
            broker.buy(stock, 100);
        }else{
            broker.sell(stock, 10);
        }

    }

}
```

We will create a mock for the StockBroker.getQoute method that takes a Stock object. We would like to make this method conditional. If it is a blue-chip stock, the current price will be higher than the old price, or else it will be lower.

How would we identify a blue-chip share? Okay, if the stock ID is SBI or HDFC, we will consider them as blue-chip stocks.

Let us create a custom matcher to identify blue chip shares. The following code shows a custom argument matcher:

```
class BlueChipStockMatcher extends  ArgumentMatcher<Stock>{

    @Override
    public boolean matches(Object argument) {
      Stock myStock = (Stock)argument;
        return "SBI".equals(myStock.getId()) ||
              "HDFC".equals(myStock.getId());
    }
}
```

The code in the following screenshot uses the custom matcher to sell shares:

```
public class StockListenerTest {
    StockListener listener;

    @Mock StockBroker stockBroker;
    @Before
    public void setup() {
        MockitoAnnotations.initMocks(this);
        listener = new StockListener(stockBroker);
    }

    @Test
    public void sells_BlueChip_Stocks() throws Exception {
        when(stockBroker.getQoute(argThat(new BlueChipStockMatcher()))).thenReturn(1000.00);
        listener.takeAction(new Stock("SBI", 500.00));
        verify(stockBroker).sell(isA(Stock.class), anyInt());
    }
}
```

In the preceding code, we passed SBI as a stock. So, the matcher identified it as BlueChip and the argument matched; so, the mock object returned the quote as 1000.00. This is higher than the stock value 500.00. Therefore the StockListener object sold the stock.

Following is a custom matcher example to buy a share:

```
@Test
public void buys_low_Stocks() throws Exception {
    when(stockBroker.getQoute(argThat(new BlueChipStockMatcher()))).thenReturn(1000.00);
    listener.takeAction(new Stock("XYZ", 500.00));
    verify(stockBroker).buy(isA(Stock.class), anyInt());
}
```

When we pass "XYZ" stock ID to the matcher, the argument doesn't match BlueChipStock. So, the mock object returns the default return value 0.00 and the listener class buys the share.

Throwing exceptions

Unit tests are not meant only for happy paths. We should test our code for the failure conditions. Mockito provides an API to raise errors during testing. Suppose we are testing a flow where we compute some value and then print it to a printer—if the printer is not configured or a network error happens or the page is not loaded, the system throws exceptions. We can test this using Mockito's exception APIs.

How do we test exceptional conditions such as database access failure?

Mockito provides a method `thenThrow(Throwable)`, this method throws an exception when the stubbed method is invoked.

We will stub the inventory to throw an exception when a method is called:

```
@Test(expected=RuntimeException.class)
public void inventory_access_raises_Error() {

when(inventory.getItemsExpireInAMonth()).thenThrow(new
RuntimeException("Databse Access fail"));

bazar.issueDiscountForItemsExpireIn30Days(.30);
fail("Code should not reach here");
}
```

Here, JUnit 4.0 provides a way to test an exception: `@Test(expected=<exception>)`.

We are stubbing the inventory to throw an exception when `getItemsExpireInAMonth()` is invoked. If it doesn't throw the exception, the code will reach `fail("...")`. This method raises the `AssertionFailure` error.

Void methods don't return values, to throw exception from a void method use the following code snippet:

```
doThrow(exception).when(mock).voidMethod(arguments);
 @Test(expected=RuntimeException.class)
 public void voidMethod_to_throw_exception() throws Exception {
  doThrow(new RuntimeException()).when(pas).announce(isA(Offer.
class));
  pas.announce(new Offer(null, 0));
  fail("Code should not reach here");
 }
```

Consecutive calls

You can use Mockito's consecutive calls in the following situations:

- When you are calling a stubbed method in a loop and you need different results for different calls
- When you need the second invocation to throw an exception

We need to test a condition where the first call will return some value from the DB, the next call should not find any value, and then it should return a value.

`thenReturn(objects...)` takes variable arguments and comma separated return values as shown in the following code:

```
@Test
 public void consecutiveCalls() throws Exception {
    when(inventory.getItemsExpireInAMonth()).
thenReturn(expiredList,null);
    assertEquals(expiredList, inventory.getItemsExpireInAMonth());
    assertEquals(null, inventory.getItemsExpireInAMonth());
 }
```

See, `thenReturn` is taking two values; the first call will return `expiredList`, then onwards each call will return null.

This can be achieved in another way—Mockito methods return stub objects and follow a builder pattern to make a chain of calls:

```
when(inventory.getItemsExpireInAMonth()).thenReturn(expiredList).
thenReturn(null).thenThrow()
can be combined with thenReturn() to throw exception and return value
when(inventory.getItemsExpireInAMonth()).thenThrow
(…).thenReturn(null)
```

Stubbing with callbacks – using the Answer class

A stubbed method returns a hardcoded value during the method invocation; but if we need to compute something and return a dynamic result, the answer or callbacks are used.

Answers allows stubbing with the generic `Answer` interface. This is a callback; when a stubbed method on a mock object is invoked, the `answer(InvocationOnMock invocation)` method of the `Answer` object is called. This `Answer` object's `answer()` method returns the actual object.

The call is similar to `thenReturn()` and `thenThrow()`:

```
when(mock.someMethod()).thenAnswer(new Answer() {…});
```

The `Answer` interface looks like this:

```
public interface Answer<T> {
    T answer(InvocationOnMock invocation) throws Throwable;
}
```

`InvocationOnMock` holds the key. It can return the arguments passed to the method and also return the mock object:

```
Object[] args = invocation.getArguments();
Object mock = invocation.getMock();
```

In the blue-chip stock example, we hardcoded the return value to `1000.00` for blue-chip shares. If we pass the `BlueChip` share to the listener with a price higher than `1000.00`, the listener will behave as if a non-blue-chip share is received.

We can fix this using `Answer` and make the test totally configurable.

The following code snippet creates an `Answer` class:

```
class BlueChipShareRises implements Answer<Double> {

    @Override
    public Double answer(InvocationOnMock invocation) throws Throwable {
        Object[] args = invocation.getArguments();
        Stock stock = (Stock)args[0];
        return stock.boughtAt() + 1.00;
    }
};
```

We created a class `BlueChipShareRises`, this class returns a double value. When the callback method answer is invoked, it type casts the first argument to the `Stock` object and returns the stock's buying price plus 1. In this way, no matter what the stock price was, `BlueChipShareRises` will always return a higher value than the buying price.

But, the problem is that if we pass this answer object to any other stubbing method where the method doesn't take `Stock` as an argument, then it will fail with a class cast exception.

The following code snippet tests the custom `Answer` object:

```
@Test
public void sells_BlueChip_Stocks_WITH_answer_object() throws Exception {
    when(stockBroker.getQoute(argThat(new BlueChipStockMatcher()))).
        thenAnswer(new BlueChipShareRises());

    listener.takeAction(new Stock("SBI", 1000.00));

    verify(stockBroker).sell(isA(Stock.class), anyInt());
}
```

We stubbed the `getQoute` method with the `BlueChipStockMatcher` argument matcher and then instead of returning hardcoded value, answered the call with the new `BlueChipShareRises()` answer object.

When the `takeAction` method is called with the SBI stock of amount `1000.00`, the answer object returned `1000.00+1` = `1001.00` as current quote. The listener found that this amount is greater than `1000.00`, so it asked the stockbroker to sell the stock.

Spying objects

We cannot stub the behavior of a real object. When we need original object behavior most of the time and mocked behavior only at certain times, then we can spy the real object. Once an expectation is set for a method, on a spy object, then the spy no longer returns the original value. It starts returning the stubbed value but still it exhibits the original behavior for the other methods that are not stubbed. Spy is very useful for legacy tests.

Using Mockito, we can create spies of real objects. Unlike stubbing, when we use the spy then the real methods are called (unless a method was stubbed).

Spy is also known as partial mocking, one example of real use of spy is dealing with legacy code.

Declaration of spy objects:

```
SomeClass realObject = new RealImplemenation();
SomeClass spyRealObject = spy(realObject);
```

Spy can stub real method calls and make calls to real methods if not stubbed. Following is an example of a spy object:

```
@Test
public void spyTest() throws Exception {
    Stock realStock = new Stock("ICICI", 30.00);
    Stock spy = spy(realStock);

    //call real method from  spy
    assertEquals("ICICI", spy.getId());

    //Changing value using spy
    spy.changePrice(100.00);

    //verify spy has the changed value
    assertTrue(100 == spy.boughtAt());
        //Stubbing method
    when(spy.boughtAt()).thenReturn(5.00);
    //Changing value using spy
    spy.changePrice(666.00);
    //Stubbed method value returned
    assertTrue(666 != spy.boughtAt());
    assertTrue(5.00 == spy.boughtAt());

}
```

Here, until the spy was stubbed for the method boughAt, it was returning the real value. But when we stubbed it, it started returning the stubbed value.

Using doReturn()

doReturn() is similar to stubbing a method and returns the expected value. But this is used only when when(mock).thenReturn(return) cannot be used.

when-thenReturn is more readable than doReturn(), also doReturn() is not type safe. thenReturn checks method return types and raises compilation error if an unsafe type is passed.

Here is the syntax for using the doReturn() test:

```
doReturn(value).when(mock).method(argument);

public class DoReturnTest {
    @Mock
    StockBroker broker;

    @Before
```

```java
    public void setUp() {
        MockitoAnnotations.initMocks(this);
    }
    @Test
    public void doReturn_is_not_type_safe() throws Exception {
        //get Qoute returns double
          when(broker.getQoute(isA(Stock.class))).thenReturn(5.00);
      //returning string for getQoute…although return type is
        double
        doReturn("string").when(broker).getQoute(isA(Stock.class));
         broker.getQoute(new Stock("A1", 40.00));

    }
}
```

The following screenshot shows how the test fails:

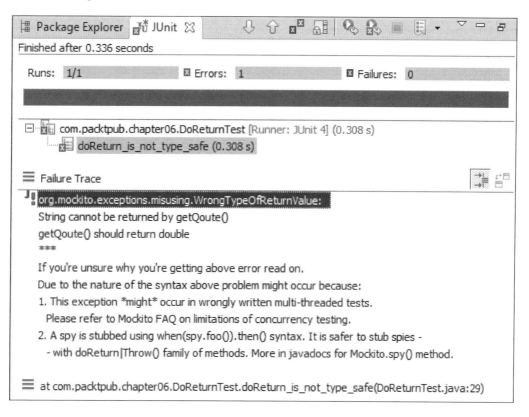

Spying real objects and calling real methods on a spy has side effects, to avoid this side effect use `doReturn()` instead of `thenReturn()`.

The following code describes the side effect of spying and calling `thenReturn()`:

```
@Test
public void doReturn_usage() throws Exception {
    List<String> list = new ArrayList<String>();
    List<String> spy = spy(list);

    // Impossible: real method is called so spy.get(0) throws
    // IndexOutOfBoundsException (the list is yet empty)
    when(spy.get(0)).thenReturn("foo");
```

The spy object calls a real method when trying to stub `get(index)`; and unlike the mock objects, the real method was called and it failed with an `ArrayIndexOutOfBounds` error.

The following screenshot displays the failure message:

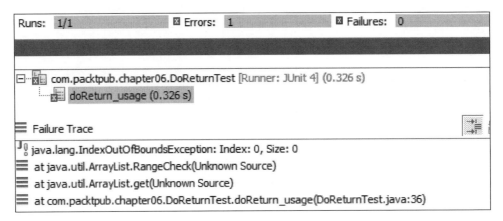

This can be protected using `doReturn()` as shown is the following code:

```
@Test
public void doReturn_usage() throws Exception {
    List<String> list = new ArrayList<String>();
    List<String> spy = spy(list);

    // You have to use doReturn() for stubbing:
    doReturn("foo").when(spy).get(0);
    assertEquals("foo", spy.get(0));
}
```

Working with Void methods

In an earlier section, we read that `doThrow` is used for throwing exceptions for void methods.

Similarly, if you want to perform some logic on void method calls, you can use `doAnswer()`. In the following code, we are implementing a logic that when the `buy` method will be invoked on the broker, the stock price has to be changed to `100.00`. But `buy` is a void method. So, I created an anonymous inner class answer to change the value. When buy is called, the stock price was changed to `100.00`:

```
@Test
public void doAnswer_void_methods() throws Exception {
Stock myStock = new Stock("A2", 0.00);
doAnswer(new Answer<Double>() {
    public Double answer(InvocationOnMock invocation) throws
      Throwable
    {
      Object[] args = invocation.getArguments();
      Stock stock = (Stock)args[0];
        //changing the value of stock to 100.00
      stock.changePrice(100.00);
      return null;
    }

}).when(broker).buy(myStock, 10);

assertTrue(0.00== myStock.boughtAt());
broker.buy(myStock, 10);
assertTrue(100.00== myStock.boughtAt());
}
```

`doNothing()` does nothing. By default, all void methods do nothing. But if you need consecutive calls on a void method, the first call will throw an error, the next call will do nothing, then the next call will perform some logic using `doAnswer()`:

```
doThrow(new RuntimeException()).
  doNothing().doAnswer(someAnswer).when(mock).someVoidMethod();
mock.someVoidMethod() //this call throws exception
mock.someVoidMethod();// this call does nothing
```

`doCallRealMethod()` is used when you want to call the real implementation of a method on a mock object:

```
doCallRealMethod().when(mock).someVoidMethod();
```

Argument capture

This is used to verify the arguments passed to a stubbed method. Sometimes we compute a value, then create another object using the computed value, and then call a mock object using that new object; this computed value is not returned from the original method but used for some other computation. Argument captor provides an API to test the computed value.

Suppose we are passing the first name, middle name, last name, and age to a method. This method builds a person name string using the first, middle, and last name and then creates the Person object and sets the name and age on it. Finally, it saves the person object to the database. Here, we cannot stub the save behavior from testing with a specific value since the Person object is created inside the method. We can mock the save using a generic matcher object such as isA(Person.class) and then verify that the Person object contains the correct name and age using the argument captor.

Mockito verifies argument values in natural Java style by using an equals() method. This is also the recommended way of matching arguments because it makes tests clean and simple. In some situations though, it is helpful to assert on certain arguments after the actual verification.

The following code uses ArgumentCaptor and verifies that it uses the stock ID "A" and not any other value when calling the method:

```
@Test
    public void argument_captor() throws Exception {
        //Creating a captor for Stock class
        ArgumentCaptor<Stock> argument =
          ArgumentCaptor.forClass(Stock.class);
        //calling a method on mock object
        broker.getQoute(new Stock("A", 5.00));

        //Passing argument captor to verify to collect the
          argument
        verify(broker).getQoute(argument.capture());

        //confirm that "A" was passed
        assertEquals("A", argument.getValue().getId());

    }
```

Like Mockito, jMock and EasyMock are the two other Java-based frameworks that support mocking for automated unit tests.

jMock and EasyMock provide mocking capabilities but the syntax is not so simple like Mockito. You can visit http://jmock.org/ or http://easymock.org/ for details.

Summary

In this chapter, Mockito was described in depth and technical examples were provided to demonstrate the capability of Mockito.

Chapter 7, Leveraging the Mockito Framework in TDD, explains advance features of the Mockito framework and illustrates the uses of Mockito in Development.

By the end of the next chapter, the reader will be able to use TDD with Mockito.

7
Leveraging the Mockito
Framework in TDD

The classical TDD style uses real objects whenever possible and uses test doubles only when a real object and its behaviors are hard to understand. On the other hand, Mockist TDD style uses mock for all types of external dependencies.

The following are examples of external dependencies—to access `google.com`, a computer needs to connect to the Internet using a modem or broadband or dongle. Similarly, to perform a task if a piece of code needs to interact with another class or module or another application, this dependency is called **external dependency**. A payroll application may need an LDAP service to authenticate users or a Java class needs a data access object to save objects to a database.

In this chapter we will use Mockist TDD style to mock external dependencies and explore Test-Driven Development.

Applying Mockito

Thanks to tablets and smartphones, video games are very popular now. No need to carry heavy laptops, gaming is possible anywhere, anytime.

Like Google Play store, we will build an online portal for the aspiring game developers. Let's call it `MockGameDepot.org`.

Anybody can upload their game, but they need to register with `MockGameDepot.org` with a PayPal user account. A game developer by default inherits the Basic membership feature.

Basic membership has the following rules: cannot upload any free game, minimum game price has to be USD 20.00, and MockGameDepot will charge 30 percent of the game price as hosting and publishing fees.

There are four membership types: Basic, Standard, Premium, and Professional. This is shown in the following screenshot.

A game developer can upgrade his/her account anytime, but all games will inherit old membership feature till the next billing cycle. For example, John, a free/Basic member, joined MockGameDepot on July 10, 2013 and he launched a 3D game on July 11. Many people loved his game, appreciated its high standard, and it achieved 50 downloads in five days. So, John upgraded his membership to Standard on July 20; but this upgradation will be applicable only after August 10, 2013.

Anybody can download games, but they have to pay the price (if not a free game) using a PayPal site before downloading the game.

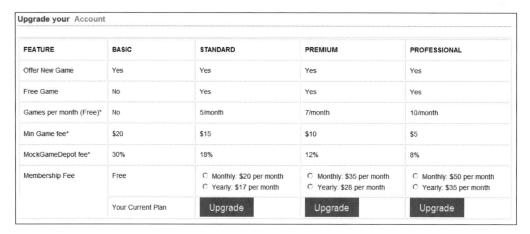

FEATURE	BASIC	STANDARD	PREMIUM	PROFESSIONAL
Offer New Game	Yes	Yes	Yes	Yes
Free Game	No	Yes	Yes	Yes
Games per month (Free)*	No	5/month	7/month	10/month
Min Game fee*	$20	$15	$10	$5
MockGameDepot fee*	30%	18%	12%	8%
Membership Fee	Free	○ Monthly: $20 per month ○ Yearly: $17 per month	○ Monthly: $35 per month ○ Yearly: $28 per month	○ Monthly: $50 per month ○ Yearly: $35 per month
	Your Current Plan	Upgrade	Upgrade	Upgrade

MockGameDepot needs a scheduler job; it will run every month and calculate the payable amount for the game developers and then deposit the amount to the developers' PayPal accounts. PayPal charges on the transaction amount and the number of transactions, so minimize the number of transactions. If a developer launched three games in a month, instead of sending three invoices we just send one with three line items. Finally, the job will send e-mails to individual developers with the payment advice.

Customer requirements

So, basically the job has to do the following:

- Retrieve transaction information for all downloads in the last 30 days
- Retrieve membership information of the game developers

- Calculate the payable amount for each game developer
- Send payment advice to PayPal
- Send e-mails to game developers
- Update transactions as settled

Naming is important and a name should describe the intent of a class. This job is doing account settlement, so we will call it the `Reconciliation` job.

Building the application

We will build the job using the following steps:

1. Create a test `ReconciliationJobTest` under the package `com.packtpub.chapter07`. We will start with a test when no transaction is performed, then the job should return the number of records processed as `0`. Following the TDD approach, we first created the class `ReconciliationJob` and then added the `reconcile()` method; but because of space constraints we are not describing this here. Please refer to *Chapter 3, Applying TDD* for more details.

```java
package com.packtpub.chapter07;

import static org.junit.Assert.*;

import org.junit.Before;
import org.junit.Test;

public class ReconciliationJobTest {

    ReconciliationJob job;

    @Before
    public void setUp(){
        job = new ReconciliationJob();
    }

    @Test
    public void when_no_Transaction_To_Process_Job_RETURNS_Processing_Count_Zero() throws Exception {
        assertEquals(0, job.reconcile());
    }

}
```

Notice that the `reconcile()` method is returning `0`:

```
public class ReconciliationJob {

    public int reconcile() {
        return 0;
    }

}
```

The test is running fine; now add another test to verify when a transaction takes place, then the processing count returns 1. When it returns 1 from `reconcile()`, the first test fails. We need a mechanism to get the unsettled transactions within the last 30 days. The job should read this from the database, we don't want to interact with the DB, which will make our test a slow test. So, we will create an interface to get the information. Name this interface `FinancialTransactionDAO`.

Now, the `Job` class has a dependency — `FinancialTransactionDAO`. Pass this to `Job` through the following constructor argument:

```
public class ReconciliationJob {
    private final FinancialTransactionDAO financialTxDAO;

    public ReconciliationJob(FinancialTransactionDAO
financialTxDAO) {
        this.financialTxDAO = financialTxDAO;
    }

    public int reconcile() {
        return 0;
    }

}
```

> Note that `FinancialTransactionDAO` is defined as final. This approach is known as the stateless pattern or immutable object pattern.
>
> If we define all class-level variables as final, then no one can change the state of the class. This will make the class immutable. As a result of this, the class can work with a multithreaded application without worrying about synchronization.

After this change, the test will not compile. Pass a DAO object to the constructor from the test:

```
FinancialTransactionDAO financialTransactionDAO;
    @Before
    public void setUp(){
        job = new ReconciliationJob(financialTransactionDAO);
    }
Change Job class to ask DAO to return the transactions.
    public int reconcile() {
        List<TransactionDto> unSettledTxs = financialTxDAO.
retrieveUnSettledTransactions();
        return unSettledTxs.size();
    }
```

Resolve the compilation error. Create a class `TransactionDto` and add a method to the `FinancialTransactionDAO` interface to return a list of transactions.

> Note that the data transfer object is named as `TransactionDto`. Transaction is a very common name used in Spring transaction, JTA transaction, and so on. So, we appended `dto` to avoid confusion. A better approach is to name it `Transaction` and put the class under the `com.packtpub.chapter07.dto` package. The `dto` package will tell us that this is a data transfer object.

```
public interface FinancialTransactionDAO {
    List<TransactionDto> retrieveUnSettledTransactions();
}
```

Run the test. It will fail with `NullPointerException`. The test should pass an implementation of the DAO interface. We will use Mockito to mock this. Use the `@Mock` annotation.

```
@Mock FinancialTransactionDAO financialTransactionDAO;
@Before
public void setUp(){
    MockitoAnnotations.initMocks(this);
    job = new ReconciliationJob(financialTransactionDAO);
}
```

Note that the first line in the setup method is `MockitoAnnotations.initMocks(this)`. This line ensures that all variables with the `@Mock` annotation will be translated as mock objects. If we forget to add this line in the setup method, the test will fail with a `NullPointerException` as the mock objects are not initialized.

Another approach is to annotate the test class with `@RunWith(MockitoJUnitRunner.class)`. It will convert all the `@Mock` annotations to mock objects. If we use this runner then `MockitoAnnotations` can be omitted.

```
@RunWith(MockitoJUnitRunner.class)
public class TaxConsultantTest {
```

Mockito uses reflection to create a mock object from a `@Mock` annotation.

Run the test again. All green now. We will concentrate on when DAO returns 1 transaction. Stub the retrieval method to return a transaction:

```
@Test
public void reconcile_returns_Transaction_count() throws Exception {
        List<TransactionDto> singleTxList = new
          ArrayList<TransactionDto>();
        singleTxList.add(new TransactionDto());
    when(financialTransactionDAO.retrieveUnSettledTransactions()).
      thenReturn(singleTxList);
    assertEquals(1, job.reconcile());
}
```

Here, we used `when(mock.method()).thenReturn(value);`. Now, run the tests.

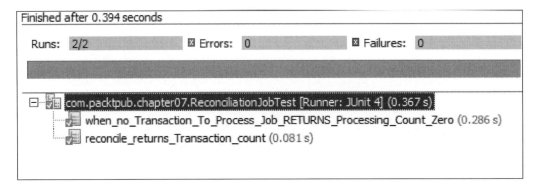

We are good to add a new feature. We need membership information for a developer. `TransactionDto` will hold the developer ID and we will retrieve his/her membership from the DB. Using TDD, we will create a `MembershipDAO` and a `MembershipStatusDto` instances. Then pass this new DAO to `Job`. Alter

`TransactioDto` to hold the developer `targetId` so that membership information can be fetched from the `targetId`. Add the `setTargetId` and `getTargetId` methods to `TransactionDto`.

Modify the `Job` class and create a final variable for `MembershipDAO`, and pass a `MembershipDAO` instance to the constructor to set the final variable:

```
private final MembershipDAO membershipDAO;

public ReconciliationJob(FinancialTransactionDAO financialTxDAO,
            MembershipDAO membershipDAO){
   this.financialTxDAO = financialTxDAO;
    this.membershipDAO = membershipDAO;
  }
```

Modify the setup method in the test class to pass a mock `MembershipDAO` to the `Job` class:

```
@Mock
MembershipDAO membershipDAO;
@Before
public void setUp() {
    MockitoAnnotations.initMocks(this);
    job = new ReconciliationJob(financialTransactionDAO,
membershipDAO);
  }
```

Add a method to `MembershipDAO` to return the membership status of a developer. The `getStatusFor(String id)` method will return `MembershipStatusDto`. This DTO contains the deductible amount for a member.

If a developer is a basic member, deductible is 30 percent or 0.30; for a professional member, the deducible is only eight percent or 0.08, as shown in the membership table.

Create the `MembershipStatusDto` class and add the deductible as a double variable and add getter and setter for the deductible:

```
public interface MembershipDAO {
    MembershipStatusDto getStatusFor(String id);
  }
```

As mentioned in the requirements, by default all developers inherit the Basic membership. So, modify the setup method in test and stub `MembershipDAO` to return `basicMembership`. Set the deductible to `0.30`:

```
@Before
    public void setUp() {
```

```
MockitoAnnotations.initMocks(this);
job = new ReconciliationJob
        (financialTransactionDAO, membershipDAO);
MembershipStatusDto basicMembership =
                    new MembershipStatusDto();

basicMembership.setDeductable(.30);

when(membershipDAO.getStatusFor(anyString())).
thenReturn(basicMembership);
}
```

Now, add a test to verify that the `reconcile` method calls `membershipDAO` to fetch the membership details for a developer. In the test, create a list of transactions and add only one transaction with the developer's ID as `DEV001`. Stub `financialTransactioDAO` to retrieve this list.

During test execution, the job will get this list and then it should ask `membershipDAO` to get the details of developer `DEV001`. We will verify that in the test using Mockito's `verify()` API:

```
@Test
public void when_transaction_exists_Then_membership_details_is_
retrieved_for_the_developer() throws Exception {
        List<TransactionDto> singleTxList =
 new ArrayList<TransactionDto>();
        TransactionDto transactionDto = new TransactionDto();
        transactionDto.setTargetId("DEV001");
        singleTxList.add(transactionDto);
        when(financialTransactionDAO.retrieveUnSettledTransactions()).
thenReturn(singleTxList);
        assertEquals(1, job.reconcile());
        verify(membershipDAO).getStatusFor(anyString());
    }
```

The test will fail. Add the code to call `MembershipDAO`.

Modify the `reconcile()` method to call the `membershipDAO` instance with the first element of the returned list:

```
public int reconcile() {
    List<TransactionDto> unSettledTxs = financialTxDAO
            .retrieveUnSettledTransactions();

    MembershipStatusDto membership = membershipDAO
            .getStatusFor(unSettledTxs.get(0).getTargetId());
```

```
        return unSettledTxs.size();
    }
```

Oops! The first test is failing with an `ArrayIndexOutOfBoundException`. When no transaction is present, the DAO returns an empty list. Revert the change, check if the list is not empty, and then only pass the zeroth element:

```
public int reconcile() {
        List<TransactionDto> unSettledTxs = financialTxDAO
                .retrieveUnSettledTransactions();

        if(!unSettledTxs.isEmpty()) {
            MembershipStatusDto membership = membershipDAO
                        .getStatusFor(unSettledTxs.get(0)
    .getTargetId());
        }

        return unSettledTxs.size();
    }
```

Re-run the test. It is working now.

We tested with no transaction and then with a single transaction. Now add a test to verify multiple transactions. This is a very important stage in TDD. Once we are done with one, we should test our code against many.

In a test we will create two transactions: one for John and another one for Bob. We will expect that for both developers `membershipDAO` will be called. We are going to use `ArgumentCaptor` and `Times` to verify the invocation. Verification will check the number of invocations by passing `new Times(2)`, then the argument captor will capture arguments for all invocations. Finally, we will ask the argument captor to return the list of invocations and from that list we will verify whether `membershipDAO` was invoked for both Bob and John:

```
@Test
    public void when_transactions_exist_then_membership_details_is_
retrieved_for_e
    ach_developer()
            throws Exception {
        List<TransactionDto> multipleTxs = new
            ArrayList<TransactionDto>();
        TransactionDto johnsTransaction = new TransactionDto();
        String johnsDeveloperId = "john001";
        johnsTransaction.setTargetId(johnsDeveloperId);
```

```
        TransactionDto bobsTransaction = new TransactionDto();
        String bobsDeveloperId = "bob999";
        bobsTransaction.setTargetId(bobsDeveloperId);

        multipleTxs.add(johnsTransaction);
        multipleTxs.add(bobsTransaction);

        when(financialTransactionDAO.
         retrieveUnSettledTransactions())
                .thenReturn(multipleTxs);

        assertEquals(2, job.reconcile());

    ArgumentCaptor<String> argCaptor =
    ArgumentCaptor.forClass(String.class);

    verify(membershipDAO, new
        Times(2)).getStatusFor(argCaptor.capture());

        List<String> passedValues = argCaptor.getAllValues();

    assertEquals(johnsDeveloperId, passedValues.get(0));
    assertEquals(bobsDeveloperId, passedValues.get(1));

    }
```

The test will fail. Our `reconcile()` method passes only the zeroth value of the transaction. We need to modify code to loop through the transaction list so that for each transaction `membershipDAO` is invoked. In this test for John and Bob, code will be changed to the following:

```
public int reconcile() {
        List<TransactionDto> unSettledTxs = financialTxDAO
                .retrieveUnSettledTransactions();

        for (TransactionDto transactionDto : unSettledTxs) {
            MembershipStatusDto membership = membershipDAO
                .getStatusFor(transactionDto.getTargetId());
        }

        return unSettledTxs.size();
    }
```

Run the test suite. It will be green.

Now time to add a new feature: Calculation of payable amount and send to `PayPal`. `PayPal` provides RESTful APIs and express checkout options for application to `PayPal` communication. We will mock out `PayPal` integration and call a façade—name it `PayPalFacade`.

Add a test to verify that the PayPal is invoked. We created the `PayPalFacade` interface and passed it to the `job` constructor:

```
@Mock PayPalFacade payPalFacade;
@Before
public void setUp(){
    MockitoAnnotations.initMocks(this);
    job = new ReconciliationJob(financialTransactionDAO,
membershipDAO, payPalFacade);
}
```

Modify `TransactionDto` to hold `payPalId` of the developer and the amount of transactions (game price):

```
public class TransactionDto {

    private String targetId;
    private String targetPayPalId;
    private double amount;
    //getter & setters
}
```

`PayPalFacade` will take a request object to pass `targetPayPalId`, total amount, and description. Call it `PaymentAdviceDto`. Create the DTO with all fields:

```
public class PaymentAdviceDto {
    private final double amount;
    private final String targetPayPalId;
    private final String desc;

    public PaymentAdviceDto(double amount, String targetPayPalId,
                    String desc) {
        this.amount = amount;
        this.targetPayPalId = targetPayPalId;
        this.desc = desc;
    }
```

In the test, verify that the advice was sent. Create a transaction list for David, a developer. The createTxDto(...) method creates a TransactionDto instance from the developer ID, PayPal ID, and game price:

```
@Test
public void when_transaction_exists_Then_sends_Payble_TO_PayPal()
        throws Exception {
    List<TransactionDto> davidsTransactionList =
new ArrayList<TransactionDto>();

        String davidsDeveloperId = "dev999";
        String davidsPayPalId = "david@paypal.com";
        double davidsSuperMarioGamePrice = 100.00;

        davidsTransactionList.add(createTxDto
            (davidsDeveloperId,davidsPayPalId,
             davidsSuperMarioGamePrice));

        when(financialTransactionDAO.
                retrieveUnSettledTransactions())
            .thenReturn(davidsTransactionList);

        assertEquals(1, job.reconcile());
     verify(payPalFacade).sendAdvice(isA(PaymentAdviceDto.class));
    }
```

The test will fail to verify the call. Add the code to call the facade with a PaymentAdviceDto instance:

```
public int reconcile() {
    List<TransactionDto> unSettledTxs = financialTxDAO
            .retrieveUnSettledTransactions();

    for (TransactionDto transactionDto : unSettledTxs) {
        MembershipStatusDto membership = membershipDAO
            .getStatusFor(transactionDto.getTargetId());

    payPalFacade.sendAdvice(new PaymentAdviceDto(0.00,
            transactionDto.getTargetPayPalId(),
            "Post payment for developer "+
                transactionDto.getTargetId()));
    }

    return unSettledTxs.size();
}
```

The test will pass now. Now it's time to add a new capability.

Are we missing anything? Yes. We need to calculate the amount payable. How do we test this? Stub MemebershipDAO to return a Basic membership dto object. This means 30 percent is deductable from the original game price.

If the game price is USD 100.00, then PayPal payment advice should be USD 70.00. Use Mockito's ArgumentCaptor method to verify that:

```
@Test
public void calculates_payable() throws Exception {
        List<TransactionDto> ronaldosTransactions =
new ArrayList<TransactionDto>();

        String ronaldosDeveloperId = "ronaldo007";
        String ronaldosPayPalId = "Ronaldo@RealMdrid.com";
        double ronaldosSoccerFee = 100.00;

        ronaldosTransactions.add(createTxDto
          (ronaldosDeveloperId,ronaldosPayPalId,
          ronaldosSoccerFee));

        when(financialTransactionDAO.
            retrieveUnSettledTransactions())
                .thenReturn(ronaldosTransactions);

        assertEquals(1, job.reconcile());

        ArgumentCaptor<PaymentAdviceDto> calculatedAdvice =
            ArgumentCaptor.forClass(PaymentAdviceDto.class);

        verify(payPalFacade).
  sendAdvice(calculatedAdvice.capture());

        assertTrue(70.00 ==
  calculatedAdvice.getValue().getAmount());
      }
```

The test will fail since the calculation is never done in code. Modify the code to return 70. Then add another test with the transaction amount USD 200.00 and check that it returned USD 140.00.

The following screenshot shows the failing test:

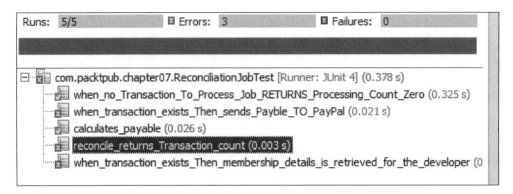

Finally, derive the formula—transactionDto.getAmount() – transactionDto.getAmount() * membership.getDeductable();

This test will pass.

The code will look like the following code snippet:

```
for (TransactionDto transactionDto : unSettledTxs) {

double payableAmount = transactionDto.getAmount() –
  transactionDto.getAmount() * membership.getDeductable();

payPalFacade.sendAdvice(new PaymentAdviceDto(payableAmount,
transactionDto.getTargetPayPalId(), "Post payment for developer "+
transactionDto.getTargetId()));

}
```

Okay, now it's time to test multiple transactions—one with USD 200.00 and another with USD 150.00, and Standard and Premium memberships. The deductable is 15 percent and 10 percent respectively. The memberShip **(double** percent**)** method creates membershipStatusDto. Stub the membershipDAO instance to return membership deductable 15 percent for John and 10 percent for Dave. Use ArgumentCaptor to capture the PayPalFacade call. Then, verify that the correct deductable was computed and passed to facade for both the developers:

```
@Test
public void calculates_payable_with_multiple_Transaction() throws
Exception {
        List<TransactionDto> transactionList =
new ArrayList<TransactionDto>();
```

```
        String johnsDeveloperId = "john001";
        String johnsPayPalId = "john@gmail.com";
        double johnsGameFee = 200;

        transactionList.add(createTxDto
(johnsDeveloperId, johnsPayPalId, johnsGameFee));

String davesDeveloperId = "dave888";
        String davesPayPalId = "IamDave009@yahoo.co.uk";
        int davesGameFee = 150;

        transactionList.add(createTxDto
(davesDeveloperId, davesPayPalId, davesGameFee));

        when(financialTransactionDAO.
retrieveUnSettledTransactions())
                .thenReturn(transactionList);

        when(membershipDAO.getStatusFor(eq(johnsDeveloperId))).
            thenReturn(memberShip(.15));

        when(membershipDAO.getStatusFor(eq(davesDeveloperId))).
            thenReturn(memberShip(.10));

        assertEquals(2, job.reconcile());

ArgumentCaptor<PaymentAdviceDto> calculatedAdvice
 = ArgumentCaptor                      .forClass(PaymentAdviceDto.
class);

verify(payPalFacade, new Times(2)).sendAdvice(
                calculatedAdvice.capture());

assertTrue(170.00 == calculatedAdvice.getAllValues().
get(0).getAmount());

assertTrue(135.00 == calculatedAdvice.getAllValues()
.get(1).getAmount());
    }
```

Now add a new capability to update transactions and send e-mails. You can follow the same strategy we used earlier. Mock `MailSender` and stub the update method of the DAO.

One thing is still missing. How can we minimize the PayPal Transactions?

If a developer develops two games, we should invoke `PayPal` facade only once not twice. PayPal charges against each transaction and also multiple transaction calls can create performance issues.

Add a test for the developer Janet, who has two games: **FishPond** and **TicTacToe**. Default membership is Basic, with 30 percent deductable.

The test will look like the following code snippet:

```
@Test
public void calculates_payable_with_multiple_Transaction_For_same_
developer()
            throws Exception {
        List<TransactionDto> janetsGameFees =
 new ArrayList<TransactionDto>();

        String janetsDeveloperId = "janet12567";
        String janetsPayPalId = "JanetTheJUnitGuru@gmail.com";
        double fishPondGameFee = 200;
        double ticTacToeGameFee = 100;

        janetsGameFees.add(createTxDto
  (janetsDeveloperId, janetsPayPalId, fishPondGameFee));

janetsGameFees.add(createTxDto
(janetsDeveloperId, janetsPayPalId, ticTacToeGameFee));

        when(financialTransactionDAO.
retrieveUnSettledTransactions())
                .thenReturn(janetsGameFees);

        assertEquals(2, job.reconcile());

ArgumentCaptor<PaymentAdviceDto> calculatedAdvice
= ArgumentCaptor
                .forClass(PaymentAdviceDto.class);

        verify(payPalFacade, new Times(1)).
sendAdvice(calculatedAdvice.capture());

        assertTrue(210.00 == calculatedAdvice.getValue().getAmount());

    }
```

This test fails since the code is written for each transaction, but we need developer-wise transactions. So, collect developer-wise transactions and then send to paypal.

The following code rewrites the reconcile() method:

```
public int reconcile() {
  List<TransactionDto> unSettledTxs = financialTxDAO
                  .retrieveUnSettledTransactions();
Map<String, List<TransactionDto>> developerTxMap = new
LinkedHashMap<String, List<TransactionDto>>();

  //Setting a developer wise Transaction map.
  for (TransactionDto transactionDto : unSettledTxs) {
List<TransactionDto> transactions = developerTxMap
                  .get(transactionDto.getTargetId());
  if (transactions == null) {
    transactions = new ArrayList<TransactionDto>();
    }
    transactions.add(transactionDto);
  developerTxMap.put(transactionDto.getTargetId(), transactions);
  }

  //Looping through the developer Id , only once paypal is called
  for (String developerId : developerTxMap.keySet()) {
MembershipStatusDto membership = membershipDAO
                  .getStatusFor(developerId);
String payPalId = null;
double totalTxAmount = 0.00;
for (TransactionDto tx : developerTxMap.get(developerId)) {
        totalTxAmount += tx.getAmount();
        payPalId = tx.getTargetPayPalId();
}
double payableAmount = totalTxAmount - totalTxAmount
                  * membership.getDeductable();
payPalFacade.sendAdvice(new PaymentAdviceDto(payableAmount,
                  payPalId, null));
  }
return unSettledTxs.size();
}
```

Note that we are using the double datatype in the monetary calculation. You should never use double for monetary types because of subtle rounding errors. Use `BigDecimal` or `Joda Money`.

I have intentionally omitted a few portions of the code due to space constraints, please download the code bundle for further details.

Summary

In this chapter, we explored Test-Driven Development using Mockito. All external dependencies were mocked using Mockito APIs. E-mail service and `PayPal` are examples of external dependencies. `PayPal` provides RESTful and classic APIs for application-to-application communication. For details visit the `PayPal` developer Wiki. Following is the `PayPal` developer's sandbox link: `https://www.sandbox.paypal.com/home`

In the next chapter we will explore design principles and patterns, and refactor code smells applying design patterns.

8
World of Patterns

In this chapter we will cover the following topics:

- Characteristics of a bad design
- Design principles
- Design patterns
- Applying patterns

Characteristics of a bad design

According to Robert Martin, there are three important characteristics of a bad design:

- **Rigidity**: The code is difficult to change. A simple change affects many parts of the system.

  A change in one place causes a ripple effect, and adding a new field in UI needs modification in the view layer, business logic layer, and database layer.

- **Fragility**: Every time a change is made in one place/module, the change breaks a different module. The change is not local to that module; hence, maintenance becomes a nightmare. A fix for one issue causes failure in another place.

  For example, a change in a local API in module A should not cause problems for module B. Module B should only know about the public API of module A.

- **Immobility**: Immobility is the inability to re-use a component/software. The component comes with a baggage. The effort to separate wanted parts from the baggage is higher than duplicating the behavior or redesigning the component. So reusability is compromised.

  For example, there is an existing security module for the payroll system, but this cannot be used for the order module because the security module is almost an integrated part of the payroll, maybe directly accessing payroll database tables to get user information.

If a design exhibits any of these qualities, the design is bad.

Design principles

Design principles are a set of guidelines that help to avoid bad design.

At a higher level, the design guidelines are:

- **Modularity**: It is a logical partitioning that allows complex software to be manageable. Partitioning can be based on similar functionalities, similar domain objects (in a healthcare system, the modules could be a patient management module, a financial/payment module, and so on), or other criteria.
- **High cohesion**: It is the responsibility of a single module (class). If a class is doing tax calculation, sending e-mails, and formatting user input, then the cohesion is less, which indicates that multiple things/activities are being done. High cohesion indicates doing only a particular type of task.
- **Low coupling**: It means dependency on other module/code. Low dependency enforces high cohesion.

Low-level design principles are:

- **Open/Closed principle**: Code should be open for extensions but closed for modifications. A template method and strategy pattern can be used. A simple example is a class creating and returning enemies for a video game. Consider the following code snippet:

  ```
  if(gameLevel == 2){ return RedDragon();}
  else if(gameLevel == 3) { return PandoraOmen()}
  else {  return new Monster()}
  ```

  If a new enemy is created for level 4, this class needs to be modified so that `Monster` is not returned for level 4. Instead, if we create a map of enemies, then this method will be simple and no modification will be required for a new type:

```
Map<Integer, Enemy> enemyMap = new ...
enemyMap.put(2, new RedDragon());
enemyMap.put(4, new  SnakeMan());
```

When a new enemy is required, just put that in the map (open for extension). The method will look as follows:

```
public Enemy getEnemy(int gameLevel){
  return enemyMap.get(gameLevel);
}
```

- **Dependency inversion principle**: High-level modules shouldn't depend on low-level modules / concrete classes; instead, they depend upon abstraction. This is also known as **Inversion of Control** (**IoC**). A class may depend on another class for sorting objects, and there could be multiple sorting algorithms; now, instead of depending on any concrete implementation, the class should depend on an interface or abstract class for sorting. All implementation will inherit/implement that abstraction, and the caller will pass the actual implementation.

- **Interface segregation principle**: Clients should not be forced to depend on interfaces that they don't use. Instead of a fat general purpose interface, create multiple client-specific interfaces. Interface A defines three methods `read()`, `update(Object o)`, and `display()`. A client who only has authorization to read data from a service provider may not need `display()` or `update()`, but the interface is forcing the client to be aware about the other methods that it doesn't need.

- **Single responsibility principle**: A class should have only one reason to change on high cohesion. Multiple responsibilities increase complexity.

- **Liskov substitution principle**: Derived types must be completely substitutable for their base types. If a new subclass is created from a base class, then in any place, a subclass can be passed for a base class.

- **Public void process method**: In the process method, `public void process(Collection<Item> items)`, we can pass `LinkedList`, `ArrayList`, or `vector`, but not `HashMap`.

- **Law of Demeter** (**LoD**): It is the law of loose coupling.

  - Each unit should have only limited knowledge about other units—only units "closely" related to the current unit.

  - Each unit should only talk to its friends and not strangers.

  - Only talk to your immediate friends. The following is an example for violating this rule:

    ```
    personDao.getPerson().getName()
    ```

Design patterns

Design patterns are lessons learnt over the years. A pattern is a solution to the recurring problems. Every pattern has four parts:

- **Name**: It is the common vocabulary. By using a name, we can describe a problem, its solution, and consequences.

- **Problem**: It tells us when to apply the pattern.

- **Solution**: It shows us how the problem is resolved.

- **Consequences**: It shows us the results and trade-offs of applying the pattern. This is the most important part of a pattern, and is critical for making the design decision. For example, if a problem can be solved using either pattern A or pattern B, how would you select the one you need? Read the consequences of applying pattern A and B and then choose the one that suits your need.

Classification of patterns

Depending upon the purpose of the pattern, Erich Gamma, Richard Helm, Ralph Johnson, and John Vlissides, (aka **Gang of Four (GoF)**), categorized patterns into three sections:

- **Creational patterns**: This handles the process of object creation

- **Structural patterns**: This deals with the composition of classes or objects

- **Behavioral patterns**: This characterizes the ways in which classes or objects interact and distribute responsibility

 Read the book *Elements of Reusable Object-Oriented Software* by Erich Gamma, Richard Helm, Ralph Johnson, and John Vlissides for more information about patterns.

We refactor code to improve the quality of a code. During refactoring, we can change code to apply a pattern. The following are a few examples of refactoring patterns.

Nested `if` is a code smell. It violates the open/closed principle. During refactoring, we can apply a pattern to remove the smell.

The patterns to refactor code smell are explained further.

Replacing conditional logic with command

A controller class, in a web and swing application, handles different types of requests and delegates the requests to the appropriate handler classes, for example, a controller servlet or an action servlet.

A controller class (controller servlet) gets polluted very easily. The controller receives requests for action, routes it to the appropriate handler, and satisfies the request. When a new service is created, the controller class is opened to add the new capability to serve the new service type.

It becomes a mess of if-else-if. Note the following code snippet, which contains a series of if-else-if handling different actions. A client can ask for any type of request; the receiver now knows about every type of request and how to handle a request. This is violating two principles—open/closed and single responsibility.

```
If(LOG.equals(action)){
  // log information
}
else if(SAVE.equals(action)){
  //persist to database
}
else if(PDF_REPORT.equals(action)){
  //generate pdf report
}
else if(EMAIL.equals(action)){
  //send email
}
else if(DISPLAY.equals(action)){
  // display data to UI
}
```

The preceding code smell can be refactored by applying the command pattern.

A command pattern is a GoF pattern; it decouples a request and the receiver of the request.

The following figure shows the class diagram of a command pattern:

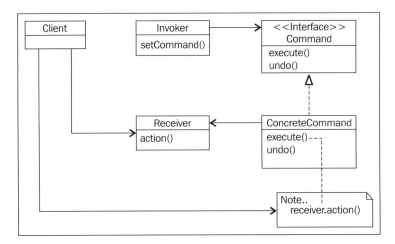

The description of the preceding figure is given in the following list:

- **Command**: It declares an interface for an executing action.
- **ConcreteCommand**: It defines binding between a receiver and an action. Additionally, it implements the Command interface.
- **Client**: It creates **ConcreteCommand** and sets its receiver.
- **Invoker**: It asks the command to execute the request.
- **Receiver**: It knows how to perform an actual operation. For example, it knows how to send an e-mail or how to generate a pdf.

Applying a command pattern

Create a Command interface with an execute(Map<String,String> parameters) method. We don't need the undo() operation, so we will not add undo(). We are passing Map<String, String> because of the need to extract information from a request object in order to send e-mails or perform any operation.

Create a concrete e-mail command to send an e-mail. This will require SMTP information or an e-mail client. In short, this command needs an e-mail client:

```
public class SendEmailCommand  implements Command{
  private final EmailClient client;
  public SendEmailCommand(EmailClient client){
    this.client = client;
  }
  public void execute(Map<String, String> param){
```

```
        //code to call client with info. Build the email info from param
        client.sendEmail(emailInfo);
    }
}
```

Similarly, create `PDFGeneratorCommand` for a PDF report, `DataRetrieverCommand` for displaying data, `LoggingCommand` for logging information, and `UpdateCommand` for updating the database.

Now, as the second step, delegate calls to the appropriate command objects. The code will be as follows:

```
If(LOG.equals(action)){
    new LoggingCommand().execute(paramMap);
}
else if(SAVE.equals(action)){
    new UpdateCommand().execute(paramMap);
}
else if(PDF_REPORT.equals(action)){
    new PDFGeneratorCommand ().execute(paramMap);
}
else if(EMAIL.equals(action)){
    new SendEmailCommand ().execute(paramMap);
}
else if(DISPLAY.equals(action)){
    new DataRetrieverCommand ().execute(paramMap);
}
```

Here comes the 3rd step. Create a map of commands for each action. Populate the map with commands, and call this `buildCommand()` method from the constructor of the class, so that the map is populated as soon as the controller class is created:

```
Map<String, Command> handlerCommand = new HashMap<String, Command>();
public void buildCommands(){
    handlerCommand = new HashMap<String, Command>();
    handlerCommand.put(LOG, LoggingCommand(…));
    handlerCommand.put(SAVE, UpdateCommand (…));
    handlerCommand.put(PDF_REPORT, PDFGeneratorCommand (…));
    handlerCommand.put(EMAIL, SendEmailCommand (emailClient));
    handlerCommand.put(DISPLAY, DataRetrieverCommand (…));
}
```

Now, the big step—remove all if-else-if, call the map to get the command for the request name, and then execute the command:

```
handlerCommand.get(action).execute()

Do we need a null check here? I would say, no! If an action is not
present, it should fail.
```

For a new command type, only the builder method will be modified to add the new type. Do you know how web servers handle multiple requests?

Exactly! Using a command queue.

Note that you should never use a pattern if not required. If you encounter a situation like the preceding, to handle dissimilar requests and nested if conditions, you can apply the command pattern. Please read and understand the command pattern before using it.

A macro command in the command pattern is a composite command that performs multiple tasks. If, in the preceding example, we needed to log information for every request, then we could inherit other commands from `LoggingCommand` and call `super.execute()` when required.

Replacing conditional logic with strategy

The same thing can be done in multiple ways! We choose the best fit and apply that.

Let us consider a code that takes a list of data transfer objects and sorts them depending on predefined conditions, and not on the input:

```
public void sort(List<T> list){
  if(condition 1){
    //Bubble sort logic
  }
  else if(condition 2){
    //some logic for heap sort
  }
  else{
    //some other logic
  }
}
```

In the command pattern, we have seen that dissimilar requests are handled using commands. Strategy pattern lets the algorithm vary independently from clients that use the algorithm. This pattern relies on the design principle that favors composition over inheritance or encapsulation that varies.

Strategy pattern

The following figure represents the class diagram of strategy pattern:

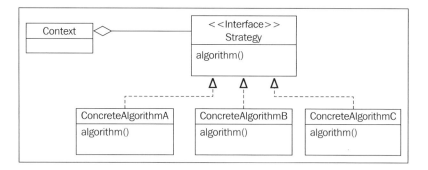

The following are the strategy pattern components:

- **Strategy (Compositor)**: **Strategy** declares an interface common to all supported algorithms. **Context** uses this interface to call the algorithm defined by a ConcreteStrategy.

- **ConcreteAlgorithm (A, B, C):** It implements the algorithm using the interface **Strategy**.

- **Context (Composition)**: It is configured with a ConcreteStrategy object. It maintains a reference to a **Strategy** object.

We will define an interface, `SortingAlgorithm`, with a method `sort(List<T > list)`.

We will then create an algorithm for bubble sort, merge sort, heap sort, and so on, and implement the `SortingAlgorithm` interface.

The following is the resultant code:

```
class SortingHandler <T>{
  private  SortingAlgorithm<T> algorithm;
  public void setAlgorithm(SortingAlgorithm<T> algo){
    this.algorithm = algo;
  }
  public void sort(List<T> dtos){
    algorithm.sort(dtos);
  }
}
```

Set the algorithm to the appropriate algorithm type depending on the predefined condition.

We can also use a factory method design pattern for algorithm creation.

The fact is no single design pattern is left alone. Every pattern has its tradeoffs. To balance a the negative effect of a pattern, we often use composite patterns such as template method, strategy/factory, and strategy/command.

Other useful patterns are factory methods, decorator, and composite.

Java supports overloaded constructors but doesn't allow us to have different names for different constructors. Factory methods such as pattern helps here.

We can redesign the `SortingHandler` class to work with the factory method and strategy pattern:

```java
public class SortingHandler<T>{

  private final SortingAlgorithm<T> algorithm;

  private SortingHandler(SortingAlgorithm<T> algo){
    this.algorithm = algo;
  }

  public static<T> SortingHandler<T> createBubbleSorter(){
    return new SortingHandler<T>(new BubbleSort<T>());
  }

  public static<T> SortingHandler<T> createHeapSorter(){
    return new SortingHandler<T>(new HeapSortAlgorithm<T>());
  }

  public void sort(List<T> listOfDtos){
    algorithm.sort(listOfDtos);
  }

  public static void main(String[] args) {
    SortingHandler<Long> bubbleLongSorter =
      SortingHandler.createBubbleSorter();
    bubbleLongSorter.sort(new ArrayList<Long>());


  }
}
```

Here, we create a private constructor so that no one can call this, and then add factory methods with proper names. However, `createBubbleSorter()` reflects the type of strategy or algorithm. From the `create` method, we are instantiating the heap sort or bubble sort algorithm and passing it to the `private` constructor. Now if any client needs heap sorting, it will call that factory method and create the object. If a client needs bubble sort, it will call the bubble sort factory method.

Always remember, never refactor a code unless it has enough JUnit tests. If you can't add code without refactoring the existing code, first add tests and then start refactoring.

Summary

This chapter covered the definition and characteristics of a good design, design principles, design patterns, and usage of patterns in refactoring.

By the end of this chapter, the reader will be able to identify a bad design and apply design principles/patterns to refactor a bad design.

Chapter 9, *TDD, Legacy Code, and Mockito* will cover the definition and characteristics of legacy code and provide examples to refactor legacy code and write unit tests using Mockito.

9

TDD, Legacy Code, and Mockito

In this chapter, we will cover the following topics:

- Definition of legacy code
- Problems with legacy code
- Unit testing legacy code using Mockito

What is legacy code?

We have heard a lot about legacy code. It is a code that is not mine but has been obtained from someone else. Maybe it came from a 10-year-old existing project or maybe from another team that cannot maintain the code and lets us work with it, or maybe acquired from another company.

We often use legacy as slang—a complex code that is either difficult to understand or very rigid and fragile, almost impossible to change or to add new features to.

 Any code with no unit test is legacy code. If the code doesn't have a test, it doesn't matter how good the program is or how easy it is to add new features. That's it! Tests allow us to change the code quickly and verify the change faster.

We know that when we change code, we need the existing tests, but the problem with legacy code is that when we add tests, it needs to change the code.

Problems with legacy code

To create tests, we need to instantiate the class in the test harness, but the problem with legacy code is that it is difficult to break a dependency and instantiate a class in a test harness. One example is in the constructor of the class instantiating many objects, reading the form properties file, or even making database connections. There could be many callers of the class, so you cannot change the constructor to pass dependencies; otherwise, it will cause a series of compilation errors.

We will take a look at a legacy code (not JUnit) and try to write a test for the class.

Diving into the legacy puzzle

In many projects, the framework forces us to inherit classes from the architecture superclass. If you don't extend the architecture class, the object will not be persisted with or it won't work at all. We will examine a legacy code of a healthcare domain project.

In a healthcare system, a patient may go to a hospital multiple times. Sometimes, for outpatient visits, the patient may come to the hospital every 2-3 days. For every visit, a new encounter is created and each encounter stores details such as the number of services used and the financial details. The following figure shows the class diagram:

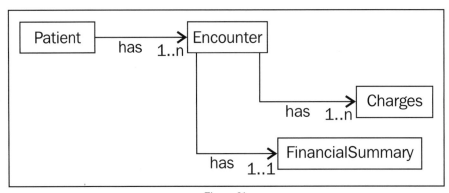

Figure 01

Here, the architecture base class is `BaseObject`:

```
public abstract class BaseObject implements Serializable {
    private static final long serialVersionUID = 1L;
    private DirtyState dirtyState;
    private Long objectId;

    public DirtyState getDirtyState() {
        return dirtyState;
```

```
    }

    public void setDirtyState(DirtyState dirtyState) {
        this.dirtyState = dirtyState;
    }

    public BaseObject(Long objectId) {
        Map<String, String> config
            =PropertyFileReader.readConfig();
        String url = config.get(ArchitectureConstants.DBUrl);
        String userName =
            config.get(ArchitectureConstants.DBUserName);
        String password =
            config.get(ArchitectureConstants.DBPassword);

        DataAccessFacade.register(url,
                userName,
                password);
        if (null == objectId) {
            setDirtyState(DirtyState.insert);
        } else {
            BaseObject obj =
                MemoryManager.getInstance().lookUpInCurrentThread(
                    objectId);
            if (obj == null) {
                obj =
                        DataAccessFacade.retrieveObject(objectId);
                setDirtyState(DirtyState.fresh);
            }


            MemoryManager.getInstance().putInConext(objectId, obj);
        }

        this.objectId = objectId;
    }

    public Long getObjectId() {
        return objectId;
    }

    public int save(){
        return 0;
    }
}
```

Every business object extends this class. In a constructor, it takes `Long objectId`; `objectId` is a unique sequence number. It looks in the memory cache, and if the object is already there in cache, it returns that, else it makes a database trip to fetch the data. If the object exists nowhere, it creates a new object. The class in the preceding code also defines a method for object states—new, dirty, and so on.

`DirtyState` is an enum, it holds different states—new, dirty, or fresh. When an object is retrieved from the DB, the `BusinessObject` class sets the status of the object as fresh; when a setter method is invoked on a business object and some value is changed, the object status becomes dirty; and when a new instance of a business object is created (which is not present in the database) the business object holds the status as insert.

The problem is in the constructor that accesses the memory cache, reads from the property file, and even makes a database trip. We cannot create any business object to test any behavior. It will either read a file or the cache or make a database trip, so the test will be a slow test.

Refactoring legacy code

Such changes of legacy code without the safety net of a unit test coverage should be done with special care as we are not yet able to know if we broke something. Fortunately, there are usually coarse-grained tests somewhere—even if it's a manual one, stepping through a sequence of web pages for example.

There is the class `PaymentHandler`, which calculates the patient's due amount. To add a test for this class, we need to break the constructor chaining:

```
public class PaymentHandler extends BaseObject{

    public PaymentHandler(Long objectId) {
        super(objectId);
    }

    public Map<Patient, Double> calculateDue(){
        HashMap<Patient, List<Encounter>> hashMap = new
          HashMap<Patient, List<Encounter>>();

        for(Encounter
          enc:DataAccessFacade.findAllUnprocessedEncounters()){
            if(enc.getFinancialSummary().getAmountDue() > 0){
                if(hashMap.containsKey(enc.getPatient())){
                    hashMap.get(enc.getPatient()).add(enc);
                }else{
```

```
                    List<Encounter> encs = new
                      ArrayList<Encounter>();
                    encs.add(enc);
                    hashMap.put(enc.getPatient(), encs);
                }
            }
        }

        Map<Patient, Double> map = new HashMap<Patient, Double>();

        for(Patient pat:hashMap.keySet()){
            double due =0.00;
            for(Encounter enc:hashMap.get(pat)){
                due+= enc.getFinancialSummary().getAmountDue();
            }

            map.put(pat, due);
        }

        return null;
    }
}
```

I wanted to instantiate the class in the test class, it took four seconds to instantiate the class. This is a slow test—a test should not take more than 0.5 seconds—as we have to bypass the DB dependency, among other things.

One way is to parameterize the superclass constructor. Add another constructor that will just bypass all calls if called from the test method and works fine if called from the production code.

The following screenshot shows the test result:

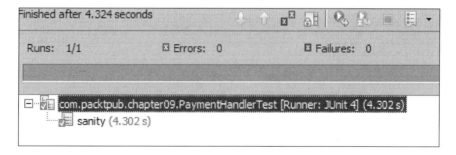

Move the DB call, property file reading, and so on in the `initialize` method and pass `Long objId` and the Boolean flag `initializationRequired`. If the flag is true only then should you do the initialization. Create another constructor that takes Long and Boolean flags and calls the `initialize` method. From the existing constructor, make the call to this new constructor and pass true for initialization:

```
    public BaseObject(Long objId, boolean
       initializationRequired){
       initialize(objId,initializationRequired);
}
    public BaseObject(Long objectId) {
       this(objectId, true);
}
```

In `PaymentHandler,` add a new constructor to call the super constructor with the Boolean flag:

```
public class PaymentHandler extends BaseObject{

    public PaymentHandler(Long objectId) {
        super(objectId);
    }
    public PaymentHandler(Long objectId, boolean isInit) {
        super(objectId, isInit);
    }
}
```

From the test code, call this constructor with `false`. Now the test runs under 0.31 seconds.

The next issue to deal with is static calls. You cannot override a static method call. The only possible way out is to refactor and move the static call to the nonstatic `protected` method. From the test, fake out the main class and override this method to return mock objects.

```
protected List<Encounter> getEncounters() {
 return DataAccessFacade.findAllUnprocessedEncounters();
}

Test will look like this.
public class PaymentHandlerTest {

    PaymentHandler handler;
     @Mock Patient patient;

    List<Encounter> encounters;
```

```
    @Before
    public void setUp(){
        MockitoAnnotations.initMocks(this);
        encounters = new ArrayList<Encounter>();
        handler = new TestablePaymentHandler(1L);


    }


    @Test
    public void sanity() throws Exception {
    //This empty test ensures that legacy objects get instantiated
    }

    class TestablePaymentHandler extends PaymentHandler{
        public TestablePaymentHandler(Long objectId) {
            super(objectId, false);
        }

        protected List<Encounter> getEncounters() {
            return encounters;
        }
    }
}
```

Now we are good to go with normal mocking with Mockito.

Another issue is that legacy methods create objects and invoke methods directly on those objects.

From the test, you cannot control the object. The best way to fix this issue is to extract a `protected` method and from the method instantiate the object, like we did for a `static` method, or pass the instance of the object as a dependency through a setter method or constructor.

Consider the following class:

```
    public class LoanManager {

        public void calculateMaxLoan(Person person){
            new LoanCalculator().calculate(person);
            //other code goes here…
        }
    }
```

This code can be changed to pass `LoanCalculator` as a constructor dependency. But this will break all existing clients of `LoanManager`. So, we need to keep the default constructor as it is. We will add another constructor to pass `LoanCalculator` as a constructor argument and change the default constructor to instantiate the calculator.

```
public class LoanManager {

    private final LoanCalculator loanCalculator;
    public LoanManager(){
        loanCalculator = new LoanCalculator();
    }

    public LoanManager(LoanCalculator dependency){
        loanCalculator = dependency;
    }

    public void calculateMaxLoan(Person person){
        loanCalculator.calculate(person);
//other code
    }
}
```

Now we can pass the mocked instance of `LoanCalculator` and stub the calculate method.

The role of Mockito

In the preceding example, we saw that when we could not instantiate an object, we added a constructor in the class hierarchy to bypass the database call or property file access.

The same thing can be done easily using Mockito. In the following example, we will create a mock `patient` object using Mockito and then stub the `getAllEncounters()` method. This method accesses the database to fetch the encounter details. We can stub it using Mockito as follows:

```
@RunWith(MockitoJUnitRunner.class)
public class MockitoForLegacyTest {

    @Mock Patient aPatient;

    @Test
    public void when_patient_is_required() throws Exception {
        when(aPatient.getAllEncounters()).thenReturn(new
```

```
ArrayList<Encounter>());
        assertNotNull(aPatient.getAllEncounters());
    }
}
```

We can mock complex objects but we cannot call setter or getter methods on them. For example, if we call `registerName`, it will not change the value of the patient name. Here, a spy method can help. We will create a real `Encounter` object using the constructor modification. We will add a constructor to `Encounter`, pass a Boolean value, and call the super constructor to pass `objId` and the Boolean value:

```
public class Encounter extends BaseObject {
    private static final long serialVersionUID = 1L;

    public Encounter(Long objectId) {
        super(objectId);
    }

    protected Encounter(Long objectId, boolean isInit ) {
        super(objectId, isInit);
    }
```

From a test, we will call this constructor to create a real `Encounter` object. Then we will spy the real object. For real methods, we will call the method on `spy` and for methods that access the database or read a file (a time consuming or resource seeker method), we will stub it using Mockito's `when(T.method()).thenReturn(value)`:

```
@Test
public void spying_an_encounter() throws Exception {
        Encounter anEnc = new Encounter(0L, false);
        //creating a spy, for real methods
        Encounter anEncSpy = spy(anEnc);

        Date today = new Date();
        anEncSpy.setStartDate(today);
        assertEquals(today, anEncSpy.getStartDate());

        //mockout the addCharge method
        doNothing().when(anEncSpy).
addCharge(isA(EncounterCharges.class));

anEncSpy.addCharge(encounterCharges);

    }
```

Legacy code needs attention. Before you make any changes, always search the workspace to find out the clients that call the class you are modifying.

Summary

In this chapter, we covered the definition and characteristics of legacy code, refactored legacy code, and applied Mockito. For details of working with legacy code please read the book *Working Effectively with Legacy Code* by Michael C. Feathers.

TDD Tools and Frameworks

In this appendix, we will cover the following topics:

- The basics of Eclipse
- How effectively keyboard shortcuts can be used in Eclipse to expedite Test-Driven Development and refactoring
- JUnit 4.0 basics
- Unit tests using JUnit 4.0

Discovering Eclipse

Do you want to impress your boss? Stop using the mouse and learn to use keyboard shortcuts instead. Using the mouse requires one hand, but, to use the keyboard, you can use both hands (you definitely don't have to be ambidextrous).

Eclipse can be downloaded from `http://www.eclipse.org/downloads`. As of today, the latest IDE version is **KEPLER 4.3**.

The mother of all shortcuts is *Ctrl + Shift + L*. Press the combination of keys together. Eclipse brings up the list of key shortcuts. The pop-up list is displayed in the following screenshot:

Run Eclipse Application	Alt+Shift+X, E
Run JUnit Plug-in Test	Alt+Shift+X, P
Run JUnit Test	Alt+Shift+X, T
Run Java Applet	Alt+Shift+X, A
Run Java Application	Alt+Shift+X, J
Run OSGi Framework	Alt+Shift+X, O
Save	Ctrl+S
Save All	Ctrl+Shift+S
Select All	Ctrl+A
Show Annotation...	Ctrl+Alt+A
Show Contributing Plug-in	Alt+Shift+F3
Show In...	Alt+Shift+W

Useful keys for TDD and refactoring

The following are the useful refactoring shortcuts:

- **The extract method**: A key refactoring technique is the extract method. It allows readability, reusability, and cohesion. To extract a method from an existing code snippet, follow these instructions: select the code you want to take out and hit *Alt + Shift + M*. You need to enter the method name and, optionally, you can choose the access modifier—either private, public, default, or protected, as shown in the following screenshot:

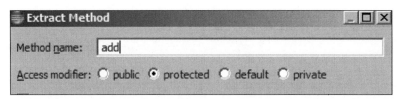

- **Rename a resource**: During refactoring, we rename methods, variables, and interfaces/classes. Select the resource and hit *Alt + Shift + R*:

```
private DirtyState dirtyState;
private Long object^d;
                    Enter new name, press Enter to refactor  ▼

public DirtyState getDirtyState() {
    return dirtyState;
}

public void setDirtyState(DirtyState dirtyState) {
    this.dirtyState = dirtyState;
}
```

  Eclipse highlights the resource at all places where it is used. Change the name and hit *Enter*; it will replace the name in all places. You don't have to go and fix many files.

- **Move a resource**: Select the resource and hit *Alt + Shift + V*. It will throw a pop-up showing all packages. Use the up and down arrow keys to navigate:

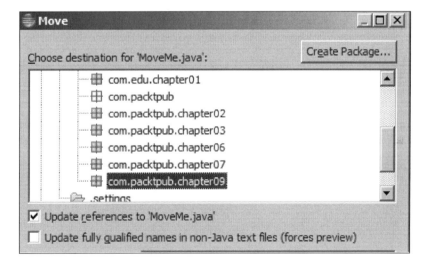

- **Inline a resource**: Select the resource and hit *Alt + Shift + I*. It displays the occurrence count and preview. Here **c** is inlined by **a+b**. Every occurence of **c** is replaced with **a+b**:

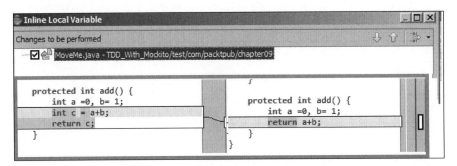

- **Moving up and down**: *Alt* + arrow key (up or down).
- **Creating constants**: Magic numbers or constant variables can be created by selecting the variable and hitting *Alt + Shift + T* and *A*.
- **Generate getters/setters**: Hit *Alt + Shift + S* and *R*, then tab out and select the fields you need. Or, press *Alt + A* to generate getters/setters for all fields.
- **Switching files**: To switch between open files press *Ctrl + F6*.

- Other shortcuts: Hit *Alt + Shift + T* and then press a key you need—press *A* to create a constant. This pop-up launches refactoring tasks. Hit *Alt + Shift + S* to launch a pop-up and then press a key to perform a specific task (this is basically required for source code formatting, adding constructors, and so on):

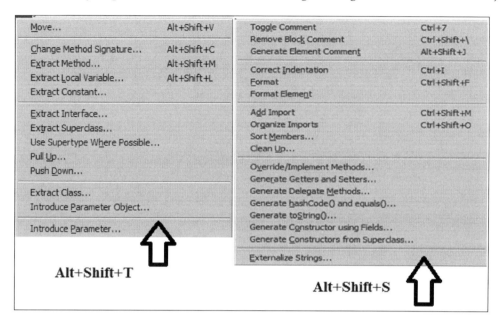

To run a test or main program, press *Alt + Shift + X* and an option; for debugging, just press *Alt + Shift + D* and an option:

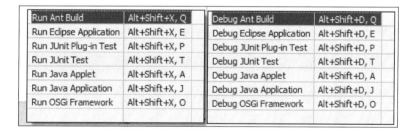

General settings

Press *Alt + W + P* to open the **Preferences** window. Use arrow keys—the right-arrow key to maximize and the left-arrow key to minimize the window to visit the options highlighted in the following screenshot. Typing is useful—check the following boxes to automatically insert semicolons and end braces:

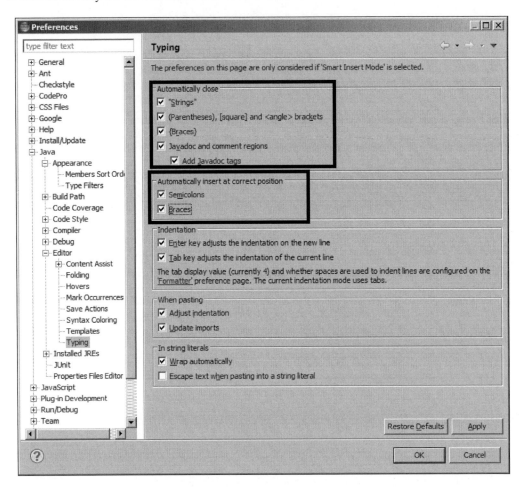

You can also configure other options to use in Eclipse.

JUnit 4.x

JUnit is a unit testing framework for Java. It allows developers to unit test code elegantly. The latest version of JUnit 4 (Version 4.11) can be downloaded from the following link:

http://junit.org/

Inheritance in Java is not a smart thing to implement. You cannot extend more than one class.

Previous versions of JUnit had the following drawbacks:

- Test classes had to extend the TestCase class
- We used public methods for setup and teardown; signatures and names were hardcoded
- Every test method had to start with a name such as test<Name>

JUnit 4 is annotation based. Any public method, to act as a setup or teardown, just needs to annotate with @Before or @After. Any method, to act as a test method, just needs to annotate the method with @Test. It provides two more annotations—@BeforeClass and @AfterClass. Moreover, there is no need to extend from TestCase; any POJO class can be a test case.

Running the first unit test

Open an Eclipse project, add the JUnit 4.0 JAR files to the project classpath, and create a simple class named JUnit4Test.java.

Add a public void method and annotate it with the @Test annotation (import org.junit.Test;):

```
    @Test
public void myFirstTest() {
    System.out.println("Executing myFirstTest");
}
```

Run the test from **Run | Run As | JUnit Test** or press *Alt* + *Shift* + *X* and then press *T*.

It will execute the method and print **Executing myFirstTest**.

Now add two static public void methods and annotate one with @AfterClass and the other with @BeforeClass. Add a default constructor and put the sysout comment. Now run the test again. It will first execute the static method with the @BeforeClass annotation and then the constructor, then the test, and finally the @AfterClass method.

Add two more public methods. Annotate one with @Before and another with @After. Now run the test—it will execute @Before before every test and @After after every test.

The following is the output from the console:

```
@BeforeClass is invoked once
 Constructor is invoked
@Before is executed...
Executing myFirstTest [test first may get executed after test second]
@After is executed...
 Constructor is invoked
@Before is executed...
Executing mySecondTest[test second may get executed before test first]
@After is executed...
@AfterClass is invoked once
```

@Before and @After are used to set up data for testing and cleaning up, such as acquiring a database connection in the @Before method and closing the connection in the @After method.

Exception handling

The @Test annotation takes an argument expected=<<Exception class name>>. class.

To test a negative test condition, exception handling in the unit test is very important. For example, if an API needs three not-null objects and the caller passes a null argument, the API should throw an exception complaining that the caller is violating the contract. This condition can be easily tested using the JUnit 4 expected feature. If the API doesn't throw an exception, the test will fail:

```
    @Test(expected= IllegalArgumentException.class)
public void exception() {
    throw new IllegalArgumentException();
}
```

The test suite

To run the test suite or multiple test cases, JUnit 4 provides `Suite.class`. `@Suite.SuiteClasses` takes comma-separated test classes as follows:

```
import org.junit.runner.RunWith;
import org.junit.runners.Suite;
@RunWith(Suite.class)
@Suite.SuiteClasses({JUnit4Test.class, My2ndTest.class})
public class JunitSuit { }
```

Ignoring a test

Use `@Ignore` (the reason being, *why wouldn't you want to ignore?*)

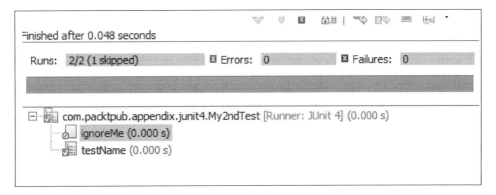

Asserting a value

JUnit provides the `Assert` class with many static methods to compare expected and orginal values. Suppose there is a class called Calculator that takes two `int` parameters, adds the values, and returns the result. If you want to test this, you can pass value 1 and 2 to the `add()` method and expect that 3 will be returned:

```
@Test
public void assertMe() throws Exception {
    int expected = 1+2;
    assertEquals(expected, new Calculator().add(1, 2));
}
```

If the logic in the Calculator class is wrong, the test will fail. In the following code snippet, the Calculator class does not add two arguments, but returns only parameter a. This is wrong; it should add the argument a and b and then return the result:

```
class Calculator {
  public int add(int a, int b) {
      return a;
  }
}
```

The unit test will complain and ask you to fix this; the preceding JUnit test will fail as the test expects that the add() method will return 3, but, in reality, it returns 1.

 Unit testing is not about testing all the methods of a class; rather, it is about testing the behavior. A class can have multiple methods, but it is up to you to write a proper test.

Summary

In this appendix, we've covered Eclipse basics and used keyboard shortcuts to refactor code and expedite development. Also, we've learned about JUnit 4.*x* basics, used the JUnit 4.*x* framework to write Java unit tests, and used JUnit 4.*x* annotations.

In the next appendix, we will cover agile practices—continuous integration and agile methodologies.

B
Agile Practices

In this appendix we will cover the following topics:

- Continuous integration
- Jenkins as a continuous integration tool
- Agile development methodologies—Scrum and Kanban

Exploring continuous integration

Continuous integration is an **eXtreme Programming (XP)** concept. It was introduced to prevent integration issues. Developers commit code periodically and every commit is built. Automated tests verify whether everything is integrated or not. It helps in the incremental development and periodic delivery of the working software.

Continuous integration is meant to make sure that we're not breaking something unconsciously in our hurry. We want to run the tests continuously and we need to be warned if they fail.

In a good software development team, we'd find TDD as well as CI.

For continuous integration, you need a common code repository to store files (such as SVN, Rational ClearCase, CVS, Git, and so on.), automated builds, and tests.

Every developer works with a local copy of the common code repository and when he is done, he commits his changes to the common repository. Then the automated build process builds the change on the common repository, automated unit tests run and flag error if anything is broken.

If a code compilation or test fails, the developer who made the change gets the information and fixes the code. So, the turnaround time is very quick.

Numerous CI tools are available in the market, **CruiseControl** and Jenkins are the widely used ones.

Exploring Jenkins

Jenkins is an open source continuous integration tool written in Java. It runs on any web container compliant with **Servlet Specification 2.4**. The new Apache Tomcat server is an example of a web container with which Jenkins can be integrated as a Windows service.

Jenkins supports plugins and various source control tools including CVS, SVN, Git, **Mercurial**, and ClearCase. It can execute automated builds on **ANT** and **Maven** projects. Jenkins is free (MIT license) and runs on any operating system.

To install Jenkins in your local machine follow the instructions in the following URL:

```
https://wiki.jenkins-ci.org/display/JENKINS/Installing+Jenkins
```

Once Jenkins is installed, we will apply the following steps to configure a project.

Configuring Jenkins

Once Jenkins is up and running, the user can access the URL and configure Jenkins to start continuous integration.

Adding a build job

To setup an automated build process the user has to configure a job. Click on the **New Job** hyperlink to add a new project type. As of now, Jenkins supports five types. The following screenshot displays the types:

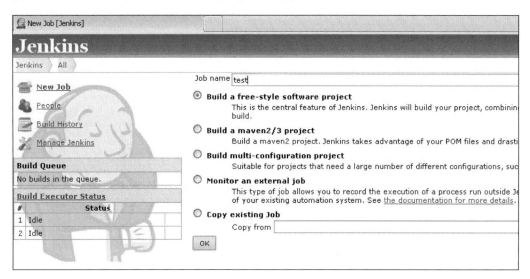

Choose the first option **Build a free-style software project**.

In the **New Project** page, enter the project name and select the default selections. The following screenshot shows the screen we use for creating a new project:

Project name	test
Description	

Preview Hide preview

☐ Discard Old Builds

☐ This build is parameterized

☐ Disable Build (No new builds will be executed until the project is re-enabled.)

☐ Execute concurrent builds if necessary

Advanced Project Options

☑ Quiet period

Quiet period	5

Number of seconds

☑ Retry Count

SCM checkout retry count	0

☑ Block build when upstream project is building

☐ Block build when downstream project is building

☐ Use custom workspace

Display Name	

Source code management

Jenkins needs to know about the source file repository location to build a project. There is a **Source Code Management** section for doing this. There, specify your source code repository type and location. The following screenshot displays the details of the **Source Code Management**:

```
Source Code Management

  ○ CVS
  ○ None
  ◉ Subversion
  Modules           Repository URL
                                            ⊖ Repository URL is required.
                    Local module directory (optional)

  Check-out Strategy  Use 'svn update' as much as possible
                      Use 'svn update' whenever possible, making the build faster. But this causes the artifacts from the previous build t
  Repository browser  (Auto)
```

Build triggers

Once the repository is configured, the build trigger can be set. Triggering a build can be done in one of the following ways:

- Triggered by file commit (existing file changed, new file added or deleted)
- Triggered when another build is complete
- Scheduled to run after a specific amount of time

The following screenshot displays the options:

```
Build Triggers

  ☐ Build after other projects are built
  ☐ Build periodically
  ☐ Poll SCM
```

Scripting

By default, Jenkins supports four types of project build scripts: Ant, Maven, Batch file, and Shell. More plugins can be downloaded to get more options. The following screenshot shows the default options:

Post-build actions

Jenkins provides the liberty to execute another project or send e-mail or many other post-build execution options. Plugins are available to enable other options. For example, the Amazon Web Services environment provides the S3 bucket option.

Suppose we have Java project module **A** and another module **B** such that B depends on A. We can create two separate Jenkins jobs, and after executing project A we can set post-build action as **build another project**.

Jenkins provides an option for SMTP setup. Once set up, Jenkins can send e-mails to the recipients after every successful/failed build.

The following screenshot shows the post-build options:

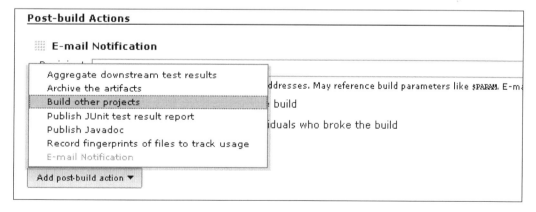

Security

If the Jenkins URL is not secured, anybody can browse the URL and start or stop a build. Also, there is a risk of deleting a project.

Jenkins supports LDAP-based authentication and authorization. We can install plugins for the custom user store. The following screenshot shows the options:

Revealing Agile methodologies

Agile is a software development methodology. As the name suggests, it is quick and supports ease of change. Agile is an idea supported by a set of values and beliefs.

Waterfall or sequential project development process is unpredictable; prediction doesn't have any base, it is mostly done using someone's experience or guess work. For example, in waterfall, project management commits to a customer that software will be delivered within 12 months; but in reality, PM doesn't have any base to predict this and the predictions fail.

Agile is more predictable—it is iterative and incremental. In Scrum, an iteration is called a **sprint**.

Sprint time varies from a couple of weeks to a couple of months. To learn more about the Agile manifesto, visit the following website:

```
http://agilemanifesto.org/
```

Working with the Scrum methodology

Scrum is a very popular implementation of the Agile methodology. Scrum manifests for a self-organized team, continuous feedback, incremental build, and testing.

To achieve this, software requirements are broken into small testable pieces. Each testable requirement piece is called a **user story**. A group of stories is called an **epic**, a group of epics called a **feature**.

A story description is self-explanatory.

Here is an example of a story: "As an admin user I can log in to the admin console". Each story must have an acceptance test associated with it. Acceptance tests are the criterion of acceptance. Following is an example of AT:

- Log in with admin user credentials, admin menu should be visible
- Log in with normal user credentials, admin menu should not be visible

Before accepting a story, testers verify the software and check if ATs are met. If development or testing is blocked for an issue, the team focuses on resolving the issue. At the end of each sprint, stories are demonstrated to customers and feedback is taken.

Roles

Scrum is a type of nonbureaucratic management. Instead of someone outside, the team decides what will be delivered.

Scrum comes up with three roles:

- **Product manager**: The manager shadows customers and provides what they require
- **Scrum master**: The Scrum master facilitates the team
- **Scrum team**: The team consists of analysts, architects, developers, testers, tech writers, and so on

Meetings

Scrum doesn't advocate for long meetings. Although it defines five meetings:

- **Backlog grooming:** Customers (including the product manager) come up with user requirements. Before each sprint, the product backlog is created or modified based on customer requirements.

  During backlog grooming meeting, requirements are understood and big requirements are broken into epics and testable user stories.

  The team also carries out complexity estimation (aka T-shirt size of the story). Pointing range is a Fibonacci series—1, 2, 3, 5, 8, 13,...

Here, 1 represents a very trivial number or a least complex task. 2 means complexity of work is twice as of 1.

Team decides what 1 is, it could be adding a widget to an UI for display or a SQL to fetch data.

- **Sprint planning**: Sprint planning is scheduled at the beginning of the sprint. The product owner explains what are the real business import features for the customers, and then the team decides what the epics/stories do, which will be included in the coming sprint. The team considers the T-shirt size.

   Finally the team pulls in stories from product backlog to sprint backlog.

- **Daily stand-up meeting**: Every day the Scrum team members spend a total of 15 minutes reporting to each other. The agenda is for summarizing the work of the previous day, current day, and to determine whether any help is required (due to any impediment).

   Each team member speaks about his/her status. As the name suggests, standing up at the meeting helps to reduce the time. The meeting should not exceed more than 15 minutes. If anyone is blocked or anything critical needs to be resolved, then only the required members meet again after the stand-up meeting.

- **Sprint review**: After a Sprint ends, the team holds a sprint review meeting to demonstrate a working product to the product owner and the stakeholders.

   After the demonstration, the product owner reviews the sprint backlog (created during the planning) and declares which items are considered as complete.

   If anything was committed but not done, team provides the explanation to all stakeholders for the slippage.

- **Retrospective**: Reflection in the mirror tells you who you are. In the retrospective meeting, the team reflects on its own process, inspects behavior/process, and takes action for future sprints.

   Each member, not mandatorily, speaks about things that went wrong, went fine, and those that made him/her mad.

   The Scrum master helps to identify the owner of each item and owner takes action. One example could be that white board/projector/meeting rooms weren't available for critical technical walkthrough. Someone can take this item and work with office administrators to allocate a dedicated meeting room for the team.

   Another example could be that analysts spoke about many things but did not document them.

The story board

Scrum teams keep a board with working stories. This board reflects the status of the team. The board contains many columns, such as On Deck/TO-DO, Analysis Active, Analysis Done, Development, Development Done, Testing, and Done. You can visit `scrumy.com` to get a clearer picture.

TODO represents the stories accepted by the team, **Analysis active** shows that stories are being worked on by the business analysts, **Analysis Done** represents stories that will be picked up by the developers, developers work on **Development stories**, **Testing** column represents stories being tested by the testers, and the **Done** column represents stories accepted by the team.

The following figure represents a story board:

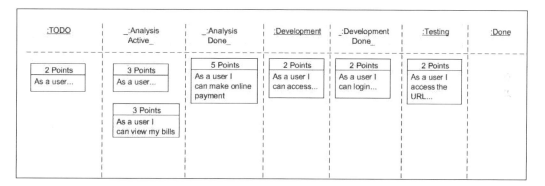

Exploring the Kanban development process

Kanban is a highly efficient way of managing software development processes.

The software development process mainly consists of three key things: analysis, development, and testing. The progress of the process depends on the progress of these three areas. If analysts deliver five features in a week, developers code 10 features in a week; but testers can test only two features per week, then the output of the software process is two features per week.

In the preceding example, if analysts and developers keep delivering five and 10 features respectively, then after the second week testing will block 16 (*20 - 4 = 16*) features.

Here, testing is the bottleneck. So the progress of the software development process is the progress of the bottleneck.

The Kanban process helps to resolve the bottleneck, it introduces a **work-in-progress (WIP)** limit. Kanban has a story board and each swim lane in the board has a work-in-progress limit.

These work-in-progress limits are the critical difference between a Kanban board and Scrum story board. Limiting the amount of work-in-progress at each step prevents bottlenecks dynamically.

Development can have a maximum work-in-progress limit. Once maximum features are code, the developers cannot take any more features. Instead, they will help in testing. Hence, the software development flow is not stuck. Similarly, analysts will help with testing when done with analysis.

In the preceding example, testing was a bottleneck. But in a real project, a bottleneck could be development, analysis, or testing.

The main theme is to control the flow and resolve bottlenecks. Visit the following URL to get a feel of a Kanban story board:

```
https://kanbanflow.com
```

The following figure represents a Kanban story board with a WIP limit:

The following figure represents a Kanban board with a WIP limit exceeded:

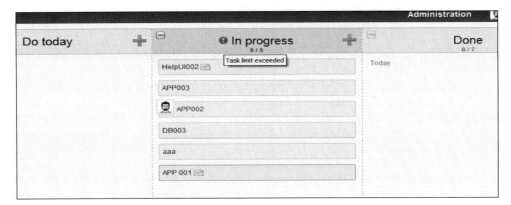

Summary

In this appendix we covered continuous integration, Jenkins as a continuous integration tool, and Jenkins project configurations.

Also, we uncovered Agile development methodologies, Scrum development methodologies, user stories, epics, roles in a Scrum team, Scrum meetings, story board, Kanban methodology, WIP limits and tools.

Index

Symbols

Q

Q2HS 45
quality assurance (QA) 13
Quickest Quality Health Service. *See* Q2HS

R

rationale, argument matcher 76, 77
rationale, redundant invocation 75, 76
reconcile() method 93, 94, 98, 100
redundant invocation
  rationale 75, 76
  verifying 75
refactoring
  about 14-17
  avoiding 19
  code smell 26
  constants, creating 134
  extract method 132
  files, switching 134
  getters/setters, generating 134
  need for 17, 18
  resource, inlining 134
  resource, moving 133
  resource, renaming 133
  scheduling 18
  shortcuts 132-135
  stopping 19-26
ReportDisptacher class 59
resource
  inlining 134
  moving 133
  renaming 133
retrospective meeting 148
roles, Scrum 147

S

Scalatest
  URL 8
Scrum methodology
  meetings 147-149
  roles 147
  working with 146
security, Jenkins 146
ServiceCatalogue class 50

service catalogue, TDD 45
setUp() method 51
SortingAlgorithm interface 117
source code management, Jenkins 144
sprint 146
Sprint planning 148
Sprint review 148
static method 127
StockBroker.getQoute method 78
Stock object 82
strategy
  conditional logic, replacing with 116
strategy pattern
  about 117-119
  components 117
Stubbing
  with callbacks, Answer class used 81-83
stub, test doubles 62, 63
switch statements 26-30

T

takeAction method 83
TaxCalculator class 10
TDD
  about 45
  defining 45
  encounter 46-52
  healthcare vocabulary 45
  MRN 45
  procedure 45
  process 13, 14
  service catalogue 45
teardown() method 51
Template method 33
test
  about 7-13
  ignoring 139
test doubles
  categories 61
  dummy 62
  fake 63, 64
  mock 64
  stub 62, 63
Test-Driven Development. *See* TDD
test method 11

Thank you for buying
Test-Driven Development with Mockito

About Packt Publishing

Packt, pronounced 'packed', published its first book "*Mastering phpMyAdmin for Effective MySQL Management*" in April 2004 and subsequently continued to specialize in publishing highly focused books on specific technologies and solutions.

Our books and publications share the experiences of your fellow IT professionals in adapting and customizing today's systems, applications, and frameworks. Our solution based books give you the knowledge and power to customize the software and technologies you're using to get the job done. Packt books are more specific and less general than the IT books you have seen in the past. Our unique business model allows us to bring you more focused information, giving you more of what you need to know, and less of what you don't.

Packt is a modern, yet unique publishing company, which focuses on producing quality, cutting-edge books for communities of developers, administrators, and newbies alike. For more information, please visit our website: www.packtpub.com.

About Packt Open Source

In 2010, Packt launched two new brands, Packt Open Source and Packt Enterprise, in order to continue its focus on specialization. This book is part of the Packt Open Source brand, home to books published on software built around Open Source licences, and offering information to anybody from advanced developers to budding web designers. The Open Source brand also runs Packt's Open Source Royalty Scheme, by which Packt gives a royalty to each Open Source project about whose software a book is sold.

Writing for Packt

We welcome all inquiries from people who are interested in authoring. Book proposals should be sent to author@packtpub.com. If your book idea is still at an early stage and you would like to discuss it first before writing a formal book proposal, contact us; one of our commissioning editors will get in touch with you.

We're not just looking for published authors; if you have strong technical skills but no writing experience, our experienced editors can help you develop a writing career, or simply get some additional reward for your expertise.

PACKT PUBLISHING   open source
community experience distilled

Instant Mockito

ISBN: 978-1-78216-797-6   Paperback: 66 pages

Learn how to create stubs, mocks, and spies, and verify their behavior using Mockito

1. Learn something new in an Instant! A short, fast, focused guide delivering immediate results

2. Stub methods with callbacks

3. Verify the behavior of test mocks

4. Assert the arguments passed to functions of mocks

Instant RSpec Test-Driven Development How-to

ISBN: 978-1-78216-522-4   Paperback: 68 pages

Learn RSpec and redefine your approach toward software development

1. Learn something new in an Instant! A short, fast, focused guide delivering immediate results

2. Learn how to use RSpec with Rails

3. Easy to read and grow examples

4. Write idiomatic specifications

Please check **www.PacktPub.com** for information on our titles

Robot Framework Test Automation

ISBN: 978-1-78328-303-3   Paperback: 98 pages

Create test suites and automated acceptance tests from scratch

1. Create a Robot Framework test file and a test suite

2. Identify and differentiate between different test case writing styles

3. Full of easy- to- follow steps, to get you started with Robot Framework

Jasmine JavaScript Testing

ISBN: 978-1-78216-720-4   Paperback: 146 pages

Leverage the power of unit testing to create bigger and better JavaScript applications

1. Learn the power of test-driven development while creating a fully-featured web application

2. Understand the best practices for modularization and code organization while putting your application to scale

3. Leverage the power of frameworks such as BackboneJS and jQuery while maintaining the code quality

Please check **www.PacktPub.com** for information on our titles